Buttons in the Dana box
Stories from a Dhamma life

By
Michael Kewley
Dhammachariya Paññadipa

All rights reserved.
Copyright © Michael Kewley 2011

No part of this publication may be reproduced, stored in a retrieval system or transmitted, in any form or by any means, electronic, mechanical, photocopying, recording or otherwise, without prior permission of the publishers.

This book is sold subject to the condition that it shall not by way of trade or otherwise, be lent, re-sold, hired out or otherwise circulated without the publishers prior consent in any form of binding cover other than that in which it is published and without similar condition including this condition being imposed on the subsequent purchaser.

ISBN: 978-1-899417-10-0
Published by:
Panna Dipa Books.
e-mail:
dhammateacher@hotmail.com

ACKNOWLEDGEMENTS

No book ever writes itself, and although the idea always seems simple, the actual work of sharing ones thoughts in a coherent way demands the help of others.

In this respect I feel blessed to have been aided by the people listed below, for their help, support and expertise.

Michael Aaron Kewley, my son and initial inspiration for collecting these anecdotes and presenting them in this form.
Isabelle Kewley, my wife, supporter and friend, who typeset the words and made them into the book you are holding.
Sarah and Alan Linwood, who kindly proof read the second draught of the book and who have helped me in many ways.

To these people and others I have not mentioned, I am as always, extremely grateful.

May they all be well and happy.

Buttons in the Dana Box

Commit fully to this moment, to this life.
Do what you do with all your heart,
and never mind the result.
Be happy.

Buttons in the Dana Box

Introduction

I can honestly say that my greatest passion and joy is to share the Dhamma with disciples and students who have the intention to train in the way of Love and Awareness. I endeavour always to present this 'Pure Dhamma,' which is not tainted by religion, dogma or personal views and opinions, and encourage all my students to 'look only within,' for the truth. Inspired now by certain friends and disciples I have gathered together a collection of anecdotes and stories that I often use when teaching, to make this small book. The purpose is, as always, to bring the practice of Dhamma into every aspect of our daily life.

I trained with a master who, when encouraged, would also share his stories to serve and support me. I found this very useful and it was always a pleasure and a privilige for me to hear them, and added another dimension to our relationship. To know the man as well as the master. I cherish those moments of his life's journey.

Dhamma is always alive and vibrant. It is not something to only think about, it is something to do. Something to make real in your life. Live with love and be aware, empower these two qualities moment after moment and watch your life change from this place.

When the Dhamma heart is truly open, we are, and feel ourselves to be intertwined and interconnected to the lives of all the beings that we share this planet with, from humans, and all mammals, to fish, birds and insects. This realisation of 'Oneness,' is the highest goal on our path. It is always a journey worth our greatest effort. Therefore the true disciple lives their life with love and awareness and serves the world to ease the suffering of others.

This is a gift to bring to your own life and the lives of all the beings that you come into contact with.
May this small book support you on your own personal journey.

        May all beings be happy.

Michael Kewley
Dhammachariya Paññadipa
France 2011

Dhamma is simple. Live with love and be aware. It is only the mind that complicates this teaching and says that it is not enough. The mind, invested as it is in fascination and distraction from simply being, always seeks something outside the reality of the moment.

Dhamma is everywhere

My teacher arrived back at his monastery one afternoon after visiting his other monastery in London. He came straight to the kitchen where I, as a monk was making a cup of tea. His smile was enormous and he said immediately, "Paññadipa, I have just heard my whole philosophy in a song on the car radio." (He was searching for a news station and bumped into pop music.) "Really," I said, "What was it?" "Don't worry, be happy," he replied.
(Don't worry, be happy: Bobby McFerrin 1988)

Dhamma is everywhere. We don't have to seek it out, we only have to open ourselves to the reality of life and look, there it is!
We can spend years chasing ideas of enlightenment and liberation only to find that they were qualities we were carrying with us all the time. We didn't see them because we were always looking into the distance, always looking for something special. Chasing the imagination and waiting for the big moment in meditation, or the bolt of lightning that would transform our lives forever!
However, the real masters speak of old age, sickness and death as the objects of our reflection. They speak of our ordinary lives as being the vehicle for our liberation. Once we step outside that, we are lost. Running after a series of misunderstandings about Dhamma that we have created in the mind.

Before we have children we cannot imagine what it is like to have children. Once we have our children, it's just being a parent.
It's everything, but nothing special. This is Dhamma.

Before we have understanding our life is just our ordinary life, when our heart is finally open our life is still our ordinary life.

It's everything, but nothing special.

So we let go, and let go, and let go and allow the Dhamma to come to us.

It's a little bit like those old 3D images we used to stare at. For a long time nothing, but the moment we relax, look, there it is!

The Buddha that we meet
is the Buddha we carry in our heart.

You made me do it!

When I was a very young man I had an apartment in Cardiff, capital city of Wales. I lived quietly, learning meditation and Dhamma. My pleasure on Sunday evenings was to go to bed early and read for an hour before sleeping. However, Sunday evening, after the bars had closed, was the time when a young couple would arrive in the alley next to my apartment and begin their courting.

It was always the same situation. Low, hushed romantic voices, then silence and more hushed romantic voices. This lasted for some time until the voices became louder and more agressive.

Then CRACK!

The man hit the woman and she cried.

After a pause the man, speaking loudly now over the tears of the young woman, would always say the same thing, "It's not my fault that I hit you, you made me do it, I had no choice!"

Even at the very beginning of my Dhamma life I knew that this could not be the truth. In every moment there is a choice and for whatever reason we choose what we choose and then act upon it. We are always responsible for our words and actions and however clever and manipulative we may be, we cannot escape the consequence of what we do.

Violence and agression has never brought anything of value to the world, either in personal or global relationships and yet it continues everywhere all the time. Perhaps now we feel more comfortable with the ideas of war and killing as our cinematic heros are exactly the same as the villains they want to destroy, except of course, they work on the side of 'good,' and they won't hurt children!

Dhamma is not and never can be like this.

Rationalising and justifying violence is a face of Dhamma that does not exist.

The basis of Dhamma is love and the basis of love is acceptance.

We accept the reality of the situation and then respond and we are always responsible for that response, whether we realise it or not. It is always our choice whether we continue to empower the delusion that it's acceptable to hurt, humiliate and kill other beings, or offer something that has value.

Perhaps we stand alone against many political and religious arguments, but we must remember that the fighting won't stop until we stop fighting.

When we think about fighting we may think about the conflict in Iraq or Afganistan, somewhere far away and separate from us, but we also have to look at our own life, our relationships with our parents, our children, our colleagues. What is it that we bring to these people? Love, compassion, acceptance or just more disputes?

Beings are the way they are, that is their choice, you are the way you are, that is your choice. How do you choose to be?

In every moment we are making our decisions of how to express our life, and in every moment we have the choice to act from love or fear.

In reality there is never a true victim who can say, 'I had no choice,' there is only someone rationalising their behaviour.

Life is about choice and when we choose it is wise to choose the best.

The best choice is love. The best choice is compassion. The best choice is harmony with life.

This way you will be happy and share that happiness with all beings.

The human mind can believe anything,
but as disciples of Dhamma
we must remember that belief is not the truth,
belief is what we cultivate
when we don't know the truth.

Always alone

At one time I was travelling through India by train when I found myself in conversation with a lovely Indian woman. The subject turned towards meditation and she began to tell me about herself and her guru.

"My guru," she began, "has a special form of meditation that he discovered by himself."

She then explained the first part of his instruction to her, but it was a type of practice already familar to me.

"I know this style of meditation," I said.

"Ah yes, but this is not his unique style." She explained then the second part of the practice. This too was a familiar meditation practice, and so I told her that I knew this also.

"Ah yes," she said, "but it is the third part that is unique and known only to our guru and his disciples. When the first two parts of the practice are completed, the spirit of our guru enters the minds of his disciples and cleans them of all impurities. This is his special and unique practice."

I was silent for a moment and then asked, "Does the disciple need any special qualities to do this practice?"

"Only faith," she said.

Understanding Dhamma means to understand self responsibility, and that the world we experience is the one that we create for ourselves. We, in every moment, are responsible for ourselves and everything we do, good or bad, wise or foolish, loving or cruel.

Our Vipassana and Loving Kindness way is to let go of the things that take us into suffering and unhappiness and be free. As we do this more and more the heart opens and we are in peace, accepting now the reality of things without struggle.

With wisdom, difficulties are seen only as difficulties, people

are seen only as people, life is seen only as life. No problem, just reality.
Sometimes pleasant, sometimes unpleasant, but always 'just like this!'
This is a beautiful way to meet our life and is available to everyone who wants it, however, the work that needs to be done we have to do for ourselves.
No-one can do it for us!
No-one can take away our foolishness or our pain and suffering, and no-one can give us happiness. The world that we experience begins and ends with us. We alone empower the conditions of this world and no-one has the power to purify it or change it, except ourselves.
If the Buddha could have enlightened others simply by touching them or purifying their mind, I feel sure that he would have done it.
If I could take away your pain and confusion with a magic formula I too would do that.

One time when my eldest son was very small I had to take him to the dentist. He was very nervous and I, as his caring, loving father, tried to reassure him and take away those anxieties. I couldn't do it. He was locked in his own small world of fear, and I was left standing outside.
We can support, love and help. We can talk, soothe and caress, but ultimately we cannot enter the world of another.
Because of this reality our whole training is established upon awareness and love. Awareness to see the reality and love to accept this reality. With the resulting wisdom we can respond to life without being a victim to religious, spiritual or social programming.
No-one can be aware for us. No-one can be loving for us. No-one can purify our mind for us.

If we want to see the results of practice we have to do this practice for ourselves. This, in the end, is the most important teaching.

> Purity and impurity are personal concerns,
> no-one can purify another.
>
> Dhammapada: verse 165

It is only from a position of fear
that we can be manipulated by the world.
Therefore the Pure Dhamma way
is to live from love,
celebrate this life - and be free.

Buttons in the Dana box

After my teacher had instructed me to teach Dhamma in 1984 on my home Island in the United Kingdom, I began to present five week structured courses of Vipassana and Loving Kindness meditation. This coupled with simple Buddhist teaching was very popular, if only because in those days it was still quite new to the United Kingdom.

For two hours one evening a week people could hear about and sample meditation and Dhamma practice.

Myself and the small group that had gathered around me, advertised these free courses in the local newspapers, hired a hall and asked only for donation in return to repay the advertising and the room rental.

We placed a dana box close to the door and explained it's function.

"This is only to help support the group, pay the costs of the course and promote Buddhism and meditation on the Isle of Man, please leave a donation when we are finished."

Rarely did we find any more than a few coins there and on one occasion we found only three buttons in the dana box.

Generosity is highly prized in Dhamma training because of it's fearless nature.

It is the first of the 'ten perfections' (dana paramita) described by the Buddha and resides in the loving heart. When we are not afraid we can share. When we don't think about keeping more than we need for ourselves, we can share. When we see the value of what we have received we can be generous.

However, whenever we take more than we need, that is greed, and the basis for that greed is fear. In the end they are only the two extremes of the same moment of mind.

Dhamma itself is a sharing process, but paradoxically, it

comes at a price.

In every moment we show ourselves, and the mind that makes the illusion of giving but actually takes and gives less than nothing in return, displays only a closed heart.

We pretend something in front of others but always reveal our true nature. The mind of the 'button person,' is closed, and the door is locked with greed and fear. This is a true prison.

Later perhaps this person laughed at how clever he was, but his suffering continues. We can mislead and delude others, but we cannot fool ourselves forever. Sooner or later we meet the reality of our mind set.

When I was a monk I was supported principally by a very lovely Burmese woman. I was surprised and humbled by her generosity and when later I thanked her, she said, "No need to thank me. We Burmese believe that what we give comes back to us three times more. With this I can support other monks."

The fearful heart shows itself and the loving heart shows itself. Let go of fear, let go of greed and allow this loving heart to manifest into your life and the life of all beings. The absolute necessity for a life established in love and compassion is like a joke: you either get it or you don't get it, but it cannot be explained!

This life

At one time I knelt in front of my teacher and complained. Nothing new in this, but I felt my life to be very difficult and unrelenting. I was married with two small children, a huge mortgage, three jobs to pay for everything and no end in sight. I felt exhausted and wanted to be free from this situation. I asked my teacher if I could run away from all this, ordain as a monk and live a simple life.
"Of course we can ordain you easily anytime you want," he said, "but this is not your kamma now. Right now your kamma is to be with your family, to take care of them, to serve them and find the Dhamma here. When you do this you will understand properly."

My teacher had a way to speak that would always touch my heart. Listening to his words it became obvious, the Dhamma life, the true Dhamma life, is not about running away until everything is easy, it is about facing our difficulties and using them for our own liberation.
It may be a much more romantic idea to sit in a cave in the Himalayas contemplating the navel, but it is much more realistic to meet the consequence of our actions and use them as they present themselves moment by moment.

Without our suffering, how could we end our suffering?

Our life is the mirror of our mind and it will always bring good results if we use it wisely. Knowing what to do and what to leave undone. When to speak and when to be silent. What to empower and what to let go of.
There is a time to be a monk or a nun, and a time to meet our worldly kamma. Being married brings responsibilities. Being

a parent brings responsibilities. Being a student of Dhamma brings responsibilities. Once we recognise this everything is practice and we use our ordinary daily life as our path.

As a disciple of Dhamma and of my teacher I heard these beautiful words and saw the problem. It wasn't the situation, it was my relationship to the situation! Once I changed, everything changed.

In that moment I resolved to be the best husband that I could be, the best that father I could be, the best disciple that I could be.

Complaining has no value at all. Running away from life difficulties is endless, for wherever we go we will always meet ourselves, the originator of these difficulties. Now, with Dhamma understanding we can see the truth and use this very moment for our own liberation.

The way to perfect peace:
Live from wisdom, not intelligence.
Live from love, not hatred.
Live from compassion, not fear.
This is Dhamma, simple, but not easy.

Kindness

At one time I arrived in the small town of Banda in northern India. This is a town well off the beaten track for travellers and I was there to meet with a teacher from a different tradition. English, although widely spoken in India, had not reached very many of the locals in this town and I found myself isolated unable to make it clear where I wanted to go. Just then a young Indian man on a scooter arrived to help me. I explained my situation and showed him the address where I needed to go to. He spoke English quite well and offered to take me on his scooter.

This was wonderful and after some time we arrived at the teachers house. I dismounted the scooter and immediately offered some rupees towards the cost of the petrol. The young man smiled and said no.

"You are a guest in my country," he said, "It is my pleasure to help you."

He drove away and I never saw him again.

The Buddha is my great hero and has been for all of the forty years I have considered myself to be a true disciple of Dhamma. So many of the stories about his life are beautiful and inspiring, but in reality, what is it that we really remember about great people, about great spiritual masters? Simply put I will say that it is their kindness.

Magical and mystical powers mean nothing against the magnificence of love manifesting as concern and kindness for others.

But kindness is not only demonstrated by spiritual masters. It is happening every moment of every day, everywhere.

The media don't report it because kindness is rarely a story, but it's there - always. People helping each other for no reason other than to help because they can. In my life I have met and still meet enormous amounts of kindness. It seems that so much of the time people just need the moment for their heart to express itself. And this kindness does not ask for something in return. When the heart is open, giving and sharing becomes everything. To offer love and kindness to all beings, beginning with ourself and then radiating that outwards to all beings in the universe is the greatest spiritual practice of all.

Never to make divisions about our kindness, but to offer it and apply it to all. As the true masters say: I am kind to those who are kind to me. I am kind to those who are not kind to me. I am kind.

This is a practice worthy of following.

As human beings we have the potential in each moment to be Buddhas or demons, to manifest love and compassion and feel connected to the world we live in, or outside, separate and controlling. There is no sport in taking the life of others, and there is no skill in destroying. Once we understand that 'all is one' we will feel connected to everyone and everything, and able to realise our true loving potential.

Going nowhere

There is a Japanese Zen koan which says, 'the Buddha always resides at Vulture Peak', and it was the understanding of this that changed my relationship with life and death. Vulture Peak (Gridhkut) is an outcrop of rock, just outside the town of Rag Ghir, northern India where some two thousand six hundred years ago, the Buddha would spend the rains retreats with his attendant Ananda. This he did for many, many seasons. It is now possible to visit this place, to walk up Bimbisaras road to the outcrop of rock. Here many devoted Buddhists place garlands to honour the Buddha himself. During my first visit to India I went eagerly to Vulture Peak to place my garland and to pay my respects. The place is in the hills, and the view across the plain is quite magnificent. However, as much as I looked around Vulture Peak I did not see the Buddha there. He was not hiding behind any rocks, he was not trying to avoid being seen. He was simply not there. And yet, there was a certain feeling. A certain sense of awe, of peacefulness, of calm. A certain connectedness with the Buddha himself. Physically we can say that he certainly was not there, but emotionally and spiritually, the Buddha was everywhere, all in the same moment.

Five months before this moment my father had died. It was sudden, and there was no warning whatsoever. My father and I were close, and I although I peacefully accepted his death, I missed him no longer being in my life. There was an unfilled space that was still new to me.

However, like the Buddha at Vulture Peak, he didn't go anywhere. He always lives in my memory and my heart, and in any moment, I need only turn my attention to him to see us together, laughing and sharing our time. Standing with my

garland to symbolically offer to the Buddha, I understood this koan.
The Buddha is not here, but he is always here.
My father is not here, but he is always here.
The dead do not leave us, they do not go away never to return, they live with us forever in our hearts and in our memories. Physically, they could be living in another country and not able to visit us, but in our own personal reality, they don't go anywhere.
This is the understanding of the koan.

Integrity is the heart of Dhamma, this means to be clear! When we are clear our life is clear, when we are confused, our life is confused. The equations in Dhamma are always very simple. Live with love and be aware, everything else is just words - noises in the air!

Sharing Dhamma

At one time I had a student in England who was a professional and highly successful clown. He approached me one day to ask a question. He had been invited to lead a 'Clown workshop' to a group of aspiring clowns and was nervous about his ability to do it.
"How can I teach this clown workshop?" he asked.
"Don't try to teach anything," I replied, "just share the thing that you love, this way all will go well."

I say many times that Dhamma cannot be taught only shared, but in our training there are many things to learn. Procedure, Dhamma hall etiquette, sitting and walking postures for meditation are some, but these are only preparations for that which cannot be taught.
The posture for meditation is not so important, it is effort and intention that has value.
Dhamma hall etiquette is not so important, it is respect that has value.
Procedure is not so important, it is understanding the training that has value.
There is a very beautiful koan which says, 'When you climb to the top of a forty foot pole, where do you go from there?'
That is what cannot be taught, the letting go of this pole, and that is Dhamma.
So, the teachers place in front of others is to encourage and support their practice whilst keeping the feet of the student firmly on the ground. Love and awareness are not something exclusively spiritual, confined only to meditation retreats and group meetings, they are always the most practical and realistic things we can do in our life. Whether we are sitting, standing, walking or lying down, the practice is always with

us - if we want it - and once more, this is what cannot be taught. The desire for freedom that leads us to practice in every moment is always something personal.

It is never my intention to persuade or even encourage my students to believe what I say, but to test the truth for themselves. If we let go a little, is there really a little peace in our life? This we can know by our own direct experience, we don't have to believe it and we don't have to die to see if it's true.

Our spiritual journey is always unique and personal to each one of us. What we meet in our meditation and our life is always ourselves, and letting go cannot be taught, only pointed to. It is the most important thing in life to understand, but no-one can give us that understanding.

We cannot teach Dhamma, we can only share our enthusiasm for love, compassion, awareness and wisdom with the world. There will always be those who recognise intuitively the value of these beautiful qualities and others who do not. This is the way of things.

The greatest gift we can bring to the world is ourself when we live our life from love and compassion, following the Pure Dhamma way of Truth and Wisdom.

Pretending to know

Integrity and honesty in practice is everything and pretending to know Dhamma, or simply not realising our own depth of misunderstanding will only take us into trouble. However intelligent we are, at some point we will always show ourselves.

At one time I was teaching at a very small meditation group and as is the tradition, after the meditation I gave a Dhamma talk. The purpose of the Dhamma talk is to rouse and inspire the disciple so that they will continue to find the energy to walk this beautiful, but not always easy, Dhamma path.

At the end of the talk I asked if anyone had any questions or thoughts or observations about what I had said.

One woman sitting close to me asked if I would explain again something that I had mentioned. I was happy to do this and I feel always that it is my responsibility to explain the teachings as clearly as possible so that they are relevant to our ordinary, everyday modern life. Dhamma is always appropriate, whether in India two thousand six hundred years ago, or here today in our modern world.

Everything changes, but truth remains.

At the end of this explanation the woman still did not catch the meaning of my words and asked again if I would clarify further. Once again I began, using different illustrations and examples to try and make my message clear.

For a third time she did not understand. When she politely, and with perhaps a little embarrassment, asked for me to say more, there was a huge shout from someone in the room!

Sitting opposite her was a man who had become impatient and angry with the situation and screamed at this woman, "He's telling you that you just have to let go. My god woman, how many times does he need to say it?"

Every spiritual tradition has it's own jargon, it's own way to say things. Here we speak about 'letting go.'

However, it is easy to use the words and not understand the significance of them. We have to truly know what letting go is for ourselves before we can instruct others on how to do it, and although the words are always simple, their application to our life is not.

Holding on is what we are good at and justifying and explaining why we are holding on becomes our second nature.

Self delusion is strong, and a thin veneer of love, compassion and wisdom is not sufficient to protect us against impatience, anger and the power of ego. This man had been telling others to 'let go' for many years, but in the moment was not able to do it for himself.

Our practice in 'letting go,' is not to disappear so that we are ineffectual in life, rather the opposite. To be aware and loving that we can be at peace with things as they are. To be powerful when we need to be, but to show that power with care. To deliberately hurt or humiliate another can never bring good results for ourselves or the other person.

Everything is teaching us if we are patient and aware enough to see it. This is always the attitude of the true disciple.

Someone struggling to understand the subtleties of Dhamma is an opportunity for a demonstration of compassion, not anger. It is an opportunity to show patience, not irritation.

Even if we ourselves have understood perfectly, we need to show our understanding as love and not insult other people. This is not a race, it is not a competition, it is not a battlefield, and true understanding ultimately is everything.

Dhamma is always simple but often it is that very simplicity that becomes the obstacle. Let go, let go, let go, how many

times do you hear this, and how many more times do you need to hear it before it becomes part of who and what you are?
Hear the teachings and be gentle with the world.

With wisdom, everything is seen as clouds passing through an empty sky, some pleasant, some unpleasant, some attractive and some unattractive, but all having the same universal quality of impermanence (Anicca).
There is nothing to hold on to and nothing to understand.
There is only this moment, and in this moment the whole of our life exists.

Teaching Dhamma

During our many years of presenting and teaching retreats at the International Meditation Centre, Budh Gaya, India we occasionally met students who were definitely working to their own agenda.

The real reason to sit a Vipassana retreat is to surrender into the programme and practice as it is presented and allow the truth to manifest for you.

This is a wonderful, if often very difficult and frustrating practice, for here we give no place for us to hide from ourselves.

Part of the support for this practice is a very simple environment with the meals being an important part of this.

The meals were always the same and so gave no distraction in the meditation sittings. We always knew what we would eat for lunch - the same as the day before! Because of this, on the rare occasion when something extra was added to the lunch buffet, everyone became quite excited.

On one occasion spinach was added as the extra vegetable. Waiting in a calm and silent line the students could eventually help themselves and take as much as they wanted, but obviously leaving enough for the others following them.

On this occasion, one student, an older man arrived very early at the line for lunch and took all the spinach. He walked past the others, his plate piled high with this rare treat, smiling to himself and found a place to eat it all alone.

This was later reported to me and I invited this man to my room. I asked him why, when he was a part of a large group experiencing this retreat, he had taken all the spinach and not left any for his colleagues?

"I wanted to test them," he said, "to see where they are in their practice!"

'Before we can teach Dhamma, we must know Dhamma,' said the Buddha, and although many people feel that they know Dhamma it is in fact, very rare.

True Dhamma is not something to discuss and talk about, it is something to live moment after moment. Living Dhamma is seen in every aspect of our behaviour whether we are with others or alone and not only in front of Buddha statues in the Dhamma Hall.

Dhamma is the environment in which we live our life, sharing our heart, supporting and caring for others. Not giving lessons of how they should or should not be and never arrogantly testing their understanding.

If we are not one with the truth, how can we show it to others?
If we are not one with the truth, how can we see it in others?

True masters do not teach Dhamma because there is nothing that can be taught and true disciples do not learn Dhamma, because there is nothing to be learnt. This is only the beautiful letting go of the conditions of our unhappiness and the manifestation of our pure and loving heart.

Now the heart, the intuitive knowing part of our being can show itself in the world and and now we have something worthy of sharing.

When we offer our heart in this way we radiate Dhamma into the world. Love, compassion and wisdom in every moment without calculating the result.

When we place ourselves above others we show only ego and misunderstanding and our spiritual life is seen as a competition. Who is best, who knows more, who can reveal the faults of fellow travellers?

Integrity and respect are everything, and these are natural manifestations of a heart in harmony with itself.

If there is 'no-self,' who is it that wants to show anything?

We think too much and talk too much!
How can there be clarity in such a busy mind?
How can there be peace in such a noisy world? With so much activity and so much noise everywhere around us, we forget that life is essentially a simple matter, breathing in, breathing out, responding wisely to the moment and living with love.

Missing the moment

One time many years ago I was visiting friends who were a married couple. The husband was also a student with me, training in the meditations of Vipassana and Loving Kindness. He was a very intelligent man and always enthusiastic to discuss the merits of these dynamic and powerful practices.
On this particular day another person was also at the house. She was a friend of the wife and not popular at all with my student. Each time she would enter the room and speak or ask a question my student would answer with an unkind or sarcastic comment, all the time holding a book that expounded the merits of Loving Kindness.
When we were alone I asked about the difficulty with this other woman. He explained that he did not like her and resented it when she came to visit his wife.
I pointed to the book he still held in his hand.
"Yes," he said, "I know, but this is real life!"

This is a common situation in spiritual practice. The high minded idea of love, compassion and wisdom, and the inability to see that the time to use these high minded qualities is actually, right now!
Dhamma practice is not a preparation for something in the future, it is the cultivation and development of the mind using the situation we find ourselves in.
Always for the true disciple of Dhamma the right time to offer love is this very moment. To be polite, kind and even friendly to someone we don't like. To offer respect without compromising ourselves. To be strong of course, but strong through love and kindness, not anger and fear.
The Dhamma is all around us and the division that makes practice and real life different and separate things exists only

in the mind of the spiritual procrastinator, always delaying the moment until the conditions are perceived as being perfect.

Many people like to discuss and intellectualise the merits of Dhamma, but talking about practice without actually doing it has no value.

Making the practice is everything.

As the incident with my student showed, reading about Loving Kindness is not being loving, even when holding the book in your hand.

The master always asks, 'show me your Dhamma,' never 'tell me about it!'

Commit to Dhamma and bring something beautiful to your life and the lives of all those around you.

The Dhamma is not found in some special place.
It is right before our very eyes,
if only we know how to look.
Once we let go of the idea of searching
for something special,
something outside our ordinary life,
we meet the truth.

Getting out of the way

At the time of the Buddha living in a small village was an old man, a scholar who was very intelligent. This old man had listened to many spiritual teachers and had argued his opinion with each of them. Although each one was intelligent and impressive none had ever touched his heart.

In fact in front of him all had appeared to be quite arrogant and filled with self importance as they expounded their own doctrines whilst ridiculing the doctrines of others.

One day he was told that the Buddha would be passing close to the village quite soon. The Buddha was already famous and the only teacher to carry the title of 'Awakened One.'

This then was a wonderful opportunity to receive a teaching from him and possibly even argue and debate over detail. He had to meet him!

The scholar ran down to the road and saw the vision that was the Buddha approaching. He walked elegantly and slowly with his eyes downcast and he was a being that simply manifested peace, tranquility and a powerful personal presence.

The old man thought, 'Now I can receive a teaching from him, but first I want to test this man and see if he really can live up to what others say.'

He ran to the path where the Buddha was walking and stopped some metres in front of him and with his arms outstretched, blocking the road.

The Buddha arrived directly in front of the old man, gently raised his eyes to meet the eyes of his obstruction. He simply smiled, stepped off the path and walked around the old man. The scholar was truly impressed. Here was an important man whose path was obstructed and yet showed no signs of impatience, irritation or anger.

However, perhaps it was just for that one time. It would be a good idea to test him again.

He ran again in front of the Buddha and stopped some metres in front of him and with his arms outstretched, once more blocking the road.

The Buddha arrived directly in front of the old man again and gently raised his eyes to meet his. For the second time he simply smiled, stepped off the path and walked around the obstruction.

The scholar was even more impressed this second time. Gotama the Buddha was the most important spiritual teacher of the time and yet when his path was obstructed twice he still showed no signs of impatience, irritation or anger.

Perhaps one more time to be certain.

For the third time he ran in front of the Buddha and stopped some metres in away with his arms outstretched, blocking the road.

The Buddha arrived directly in front of the old man, gently raised his eyes to meet the eyes of his obstruction. This time however he spoke.

"What is it that you want?" asked the Buddha.

Quickly the man answered, "I want to be enlightened."

"You're in the way," replied the Buddha and smiling, he stepped off the path and walked around the old man.

The greatest obstacle to enlightenment is ourselves, filled as we are with our views and opinions as to how everyone and everything should be. Add to that our belief systems and continually arising influences of our past and it's hard to see how liberation can ever be achieved. Without true understanding we continually empower the delusion that we call 'real life.'

However, the Dhamma is always simple and the only thing

we really have to do is get out of our own way.

To be brave enough to see that everything we carry is actually a burden and that its weight holds us in a life that can often feel complicated, threatening and busy.

But just one moment of insight will change this. Just one moment where we can see the dream for what it is and awaken from it.

When we are asleep and we dream, that dream is our reality, and whatever is happening in it feels real to us.

It's only when we wake up that we can smile, breathe a sigh of relief and say, 'thank heavens, it was just a dream.'

Waking from delusion is the same, just one moment can change everything. However, the condition for liberation is clear. We have to be brave enough to be honest and honest enough to be brave.

This is what will transport us instantly to a life where we are not deluded by what we meet or what is presented to us in any form.

We are the obstacle to our peace and happiness by continually holding onto the mind that only brings their opposites.

As always the teaching is, let go, let go, let go and get out of your own way.

When the Buddha awakened under the Bodhi tree he smiled, what can be more beautiful than that - the smile of liberation?

To be a disciple of a teacher is always something special in our life, but to be a disciple of Dhamma is the only thing that has real value.
Teachers come and go, but Dhamma (Truth) remains.
When we make Dhamma the very reason for our life we are at peace with the world however it manifests.

Giving the gift

The day before one of our annual ten day Vipassana retreats at the International Meditation Centre in Budh Gaya, India I was approached by an Indian army general. It was quite an imposing sight as the car drew up in front of the building, with the Indian flag displayed and a driver who got out and opened the door for his commanding officer.

The general was a huge impressive man with a magnificent handlebar moustache, and he strode directly towards me as I was quietly minding my own business, drinking a cup of tea in the Indian morning sunshine.

"Good morning sir," he said, "are you Mr Michael?"

I told him that I was and he explained the purpose of his visit to me.

His son was about to join the army and the general felt that before that happened he would benefit from the discipline and meditation of our Vipassana retreat. He had heard good reports of us and wanted to take advantage of our presence here in Bihar state. Would it be acceptable if he joined us tomorrow?

He negotiated the details with my retreat manager and the following day the young man arrived.

He was an excellent student and gave us no trouble at all, however, there was one thing in particular that made his presence unusual.

On the morning of the second day he arrived at my room wanting to speak privately with me. It was here he reminded me of the Indian culture of respect.

"Every morning sir I bow to my parents and touch their feet. I would like your permission to do this to you as you are now 'my guru.'"

I replied by saying that this was not necessary and it was

certainly not my culture. It is sure that on the Isle of Man, the place of my birth, we do not do this and the idea of it made me feel uncomfortable.

However, this young man insisted and told me that it was very important for him to be able to show his respect in this way, and would I please help him.

I reflected upon the situation until finally I agreed that he could visit me at a quarter past five each morning and touch my feet, insisting though it must always be in private.

He was happy with this arrangement and it is in fact what happened.

At a quarter past five each morning there would be a gentle knock on the door and I would open it. This young man would be waiting there and at the moment that he saw me he would immediately drop to his knees and touch my feet three times. He would leave and I would close the door and finish my cup of tea.

The idea that someone would touch my feet (except when I was a monk where I always felt that it was the symbolism of the robes that was being honoured) was strange and foreign to me and completely unnecessary, but I agreed because it was important to him. Gifts are everywhere and the more we become aware of our social and cultural programming the more we can release it as the nonsense that it truly is.

When our conduct is established in love and respect it doesn't matter if someone is touching our feet, or we are touching the feet of someone else.

Ideas of pride and arrogance are truly empty and when we live without compromising ourselves or our integrity we can give so many things. We can always serve the other by letting go of these misplaced ideas of who and what we are

and bring something valuable to the situation.
Selfless service.
The less idea of 'self' the more freedom to simply be.

At the end of the retreat the general and his whole family arrived at my room fully loaded with gifts for myself and my retreat manager. We had a small party together laughing and eating the wonderful food they had brought. It seemed to me just another indication of the love, respect and friendliness that abounds everywhere in the world, especially once the idea of misplaced self importance falls away.

Even if we can have all the pleasures of the senses, and all the worldly security possible, suffering will still exist for us. Somewhere deep inside our being the seed of worry will take root and grow, because only to cover and hide it will not destroy it. There is no place where suffering will not find us unless we ourselves become the master.

Accepting the gift

During one of my early years in India I had a fire in my room. I was not there at the time and even now have no idea how it started. There was no damage to the room itself but I lost many things, from clothes to small gifts I had bought to take home with me, and perhaps more importantly, the little bit of money I had saved through donations.

I was at this time teaching a seven day outdoor course at the Lotus Tank in Budh Gaya before beginning our annual series of ten day Vipassana retreats at the International Meditation Centre. These courses were free and very popular as a presentation of the practice and teachings of Vipassana and Loving Kindness. Later having tasted the meditation, many of the students would come and sit the retreats with us.

The news of the fire spread through the small town quickly and the the next morning when I was walking to my place at the Lotus Tank a student of mine, a young Spanish woman, arrived by my side.

"Michael," she said, "I heard that you had a fire in your room and lost many things."

"Yes," I said, "It's true."

"So," she continued, "I would like to give you $100.00."

A hundred dollars, this was a fortune to me and certainly very much needed. However, it was here that I bumped into my British cultural upbringing and I immediately refused.

"Thank you very much, it's very kind but not necessary."

I had lost almost everything - the money would be like medicine for an illness, it was, in fact, completely necessary! She offered again and again I refused.

This was my cultural past arising and memories of my

grandmother and her sisters after a Sunday afternoon of tea and scones in a small cafe on the Isle of Man, arguing about who would pay the bill.

These arguments became quite heated and even physical as each insisted that they would pay and the others should 'put their money away!'

Allowing generosity from another - even a sister was not considered good manners.

Finally for the third time my Spanish friend offered the gift of $100.

This was the moment when I awoke and saw that by continually refusing her kindness I was taking something away from her. The moment was passing and she was standing next to me with her heart and her kindness in her hands offering something to me.

Finally I accepted her gift and thanked her.
She received something and I received something - a double giving!

In our life we all know this beauty of the heart when it wants to share, and we all know that feeling of rejection, however well intentioned, when it is refused.

By not accepting her generosity I was taking away the moment of true 'dana' (unconditional generosity).

All happiness in life is ultimately about balance. To flow, and so be in harmony with this balance, is already a gift for ourselves. When we are in balance we will be able to give and serve others as well as making the space for them to give and serve us.

Without the giver there can be no receiver, without the receiver there can be no giver. The harmony of these two things manifesting in life is always something beautiful.

This is an important Dhamma teaching, to provide the space where others can be kind. To give the opportunity for generosity. Others may take it or not, that is their choice, but without the opportunity for giving perhaps they will never see and know the kindness of their own heart.

And as contrary as this may sound, giving this space is a true gift.

Generosity is not only giving, it is also making available the conditions to receive.

Love is the spontaneous expression of inter-connectedness, freedom and joy.
It is the way that our heart naturally manifests in each moment. Love shares everything and asks for nothing in return. It is our guiding light through the maze of ignorance and fear and so is always the greatest gift of ourselves, to ourselves and to the world.

Dhamma in the family

Many, many years ago I knelt in front of my teacher and complained about my father, his attitude to me and his complete lack of understanding with my interest in Buddhism. He had recently said some things that had hurt me very much and even angered me. I needed to share that pain and find some support.

My teacher listened while I poured my heart out about the current situation and finally when I had finished he smiled and said, "Ah yes, the Buddha also had a lot of trouble with his father too."

I could only smile in return as my heart opened. Suddenly the pain had dissolved and my life was back in perspective. The truth is obvious, we all have difficulties with other people and often the closer the relationship the more intense the difficulty. This is how it is to be alive and living in the world. Before liberation it is the same for everyone, even the Buddha.

But now came the teaching.

This is how Dhamma really works, first the identification of the problem, then the remedy.

"Your father is an ordinary man living his ordinary life," said my teacher, "he is not on the Dhamma path, so the responsibility for the quality of the relationship lies with you. You must be kind and considerate to him whilst at the same time, not being the victim in the situation. If he asks you about Buddhism answer his question and explain directly and clearly what you feel, but never give a lesson!

Don't allow him to feel foolish or small in front of you. Share the beauty of Dhamma but never permit a situation to arise where he feels critised or condemned for how he has lived his life."

As always, I received the teaching with an open heart and immense appreciation. Dhamma is such a gift in our life and without it we simply struggle and pour blame on everyone and everything else for how we feel. The truth always shows something different.

The responsibility for the quality of the situation was with me, that means in reality, I am in control, now what to do?

I resolved mentally never to speak of Buddhism again to my father unless he asked first and then to follow my teachers beautiful advice.
This plan worked quickly and perfectly and I began to see that every time I had spoken about Buddhism to my father he felt it as a personal attack on the way he had lived so far and consequently retaliated. Also at that time, Buddhism was still quite new in his life and he felt that perhaps I was being brainwashed by a cult or a sect and would eventually give all my money away (what money?).

Some months later, when we could be together in peace without any hidden agendas, he asked me a simple question about Buddhist life and I answered with a brief and friendly illustration of the five precepts, the lay Buddhist moral code of conduct.
When I had finished he looked relieved and said, "but that's what I taught you when you were a little boy." He was absolutely right!

Dhamma is not a collection of religious ideas, frozen in time and dragged out on only certain days of the week. It is a real, dynamic and living presence in our lives. The moment we bring this real, dynamic and living presence into our ordinary daily life, everything changes - but all those changes begin with us.

Love manifests as compassion, respect and wisdom. When our relationships with life begin here, we bring a gift to the world.
This is the power of Dhamma.

The true spiritual life is not a religious life.
It is a simple and beautiful life
established in love and awareness.
In doing that which we need to do and moving on,
never picking up something more to carry.
It is the true expression of freedom.

Spiritual gratitude

In more than forty years of devoted spiritual practice, I can say that I have been truly blessed by my contact with some of the wisest and most loving teachers and masters it is possible to be with. They took care of me, shouted at me, caressed me, occasionally beat me up (emotionally at least), and most importantly, loved me. To each one I owe the greatest debt of gratitude for revealing to me the way to awaken.

But there is one teacher in particular to whom I owe the development of my heart, Sayadaw Rewata Dhamma, a Burmese Buddhist monk and Vipassana master of international repute. This quiet, humble and joyful man showed me, not only the power of Vipassana, but also the inescapable importance of love. If I can quote him as ever saying one thing to me it would be:

'Ah Michael, now you need loving kindness.'

Whenever I would go to his room to complain about my life, how unfair it seemed, how wrong things were for me or for others, he would always say the same thing, "Ah Michael, now you need loving kindness", and he was always right!

Because he was my teacher (and still is, even if he is now dead) and because I wanted to awaken to truth more than anything else in life, I would always listen with an open heart and then practice what I had heard. It never failed. It is the truth of Vipassana and Metta Bhavana, Awareness and Loving Kindness meditation, the way to peace and happiness. Of course it wasn't always easy, but I persevered. I lived a life around the beautiful teachings of the Buddha, Zen masters and Gandhi, people who had cultivated what I wanted most, an open, loving and kind heart.

I began to realise through my own experience, that love is not weak, it is real strength. The perfect balance of love and wisdom does not cultivate the victim mentality, blaming others for our experience of unhappiness, it develops confidence and personal power. With wisdom, we know how to live for ourselves, with love we do not insist that others follow our way.

Love and awareness are the most important requirements of spiritual development, for without them we cannot ever proceed beyond the limitations we place upon ourselves. To open our heart and allow love and wisdom to flow freely, spontaneously, limitlessly is truly a blessing for ourselves and ultimately all beings.

Now as a teacher of Dhamma myself, leading intensive courses throughout the world, I make a point of introducing the loving kindness practice as early as possible, rather than as is in the Vipassana tradition, on the final morning. It is always the longest explanation of a practice that I give and is always followed by an evening Dhamma talk on how to take this practice into our daily life. To sit in meditation, with loving kindness is never enough, we must use it in every moment and in every situation.

Love and awareness are not things we add to our lives like a new hobby or pastime, they are the place where we begin to live our life from.

They are the opening of the spiritual heart.

Talking about awareness is not being aware.
Talking about love is not being loving.
In the end we cannot escape
the necessity of the actual work of practice.

Getting it!

At one time some soldiers were fighting a battle. All was going well until one soldier threw down his rifle, jumped out of his foxhole and began to wander around the battlefield, picking up pieces of paper. Each time he picked one up he would look at it and then throw it down again. Of course this behaviour disturbed his friends who quickly took hold of him and carried him to safety. Once out of harms way, they took him to the army psychiatric hospital where he was left under the care of the psychiatrist. However, even there he would spend each day in the same way, quietly wandering around the hospital wards, picking up pieces of paper, looking at them and then throwing them to the ground again. After some weeks he was called into the office of the psychiatrist. The psychiatrist said, "Well, I've looked at your case, and I don't think there's anything I can do to help you, so I'm going to sign your army release papers." The psychiatrist signed the paper that would discharge the soldier from the army and handed to him. The soldier took it and looked at it, and then with a big smile on his face cried, "got it!"

Dhamma is the greatest gift in our life because it is Dhamma and only Dhamma that will free us from all bonds. Politics can't do it, religion can't do it, relationships can't do it. In one way or another, no matter how subtle, the world offers only attachments and whatever we are attached to will hurt us.

But although Dhamma is direct, it too can also be very subtle and even when the truth is expressed simply, our conditioning is so strong that we need to hear it many times.

We fight and argue to hold onto our various delusions and rarely realise that the voice of the heart is only ever like a

whisper in the marketplace.
The heart never shouts, the words of the heart are always gentle and honest. The heart itself has nothing to prove - that is left up to the ego!

So, the Pure Dhamma teachings are always simple and clear: 'Live with love and be aware,' a beautiful and profound teaching, but how many times a day do we forget it?
'The world that we experience is unique and personal to us,' is another simple yet profound teaching, but again, how many times a day do we forget it?
If we consider ourselves to be disciples of Dhamma we need to hear these simple truths many times until we 'get it,' until spontaneous understanding (insight) arises and this truth becomes a part of who and what we are.
No need now to remember to be loving and to be aware, the truth and ourself is only one thing manifesting in our life, moment after moment...
There is only the understanding of love, compassion, joy and balance and their spontaneous presence in every situation.
This is 'getting it,' understanding the deepest, most profound and consequently, the most beautiful truth that is Dhamma, and allowing it to flow in our life.

The function of the Dhamma master is to encourage their disciples to follow the path of wisdom, and to show, by their own example, the true Way. This is not a Way of belief and blind faith, but of an active and personal investigation into Truth. To know for ourselves, directly and without doubt, the reality of being.

Loving support

Many years ago I led a retreat in the south of France at a private meditation centre. When the retreat had ended I was invited to give a public talk the next evening in the beautiful old walled city of Carcassonne.

I was driven there by my organiser and translator and the talk went ahead. After the talk we walked back to the car park to where the car was parked, but now the space was empty!

I said, "Your car's not there."

My friend immediately took her glasses out of her bag just to make sure she was seeing properly, but had to agree that the car was missing.

Very calmly she said, "O.K. we have to report this to the police and then call my husband to come and collect us."

After we had arrived back at the retreat centre and sat with a cup of tea I told her that I had been very impressed by her calm manner and attitude when she realised that the car had been stolen (It was taken by 'joy' riders and found some days later completely destroyed).

"Thank you," she said, "but it was only because you were standing next to me."

We often think of ourselves in a small way, continually rejecting any idea of self worth and value, but the truth is that everything is affecting everything else, and our presence in any situation can be a support and even a blessing to others.

For myself I met this many times when I lived with my teacher. To see him responding in different moments in a wise and loving way was always inspirational. Never showing anger or irritation, but always being strong and clear.

When we are angry that has an effect in our life and everything that we come into contact with.

When we are loving, that too has an effect in our life and everything that we come into contact with. Of the two, love is better.

However, here is the spiritual paradox, if we try to be someone who manifests only certain beautiful qualities we miss the point of practice.

We train ourselves to let go of conditioned ideas of behaviour and simply allow the heart to emerge.

The heart (intuitive understanding) 'just is,' and so never tries to show itself. It responds to the moment without looking over it's shoulder to see who's watching. It does not look at the spiritual scoreboard to see how well it's doing. The heart serves and asks for nothing in return and so is pure.

Purity of being is the highest practice.

Our own spiritual training is to let go of any limited sense of self identity and be one with this infinitely loving and generous heart.

In this way our life becomes a blessing to ourselves and then quite naturally, a blessing to all beings and situations that we meet.

The moment we look for something special, we are lost because we have stepped off the pure Dhamma path. We think that our ordinary lives are just not enough to take us to enlightenment, but enlightenment exists as much in washing the dishes as it does in sitting in meditation. The difference of course, is awareness.

Understanding practice

One time when I was very young and quite new to meditation one person asked where I watched the breath, in the abdomen or the nostrils?
"In the nostrils," I replied.
"Oh, you'll never advance until you learn to watch the breath in the abdomen!" he said.

When we understand Dhamma everything becomes practice and practice becomes the joy of living. The heart opens and the face smiles, there is no more striving to be someone or to get something, only the simple beingness of 'no-person.' Moving through each moment of life responding wisely and lovingly and not making issues about what is practice and what is not.
When we let go of our preconceived ideas, life itself becomes the practice.
When we are locked in the view of specific ways of training and techniques our life becomes narrow and confined, critising and correcting those who are different from us. Once we have transcended technique our life becomes our practice and so our practice become all encompassing.
One clear example of this is Zen master Soen-Sa-Nim, who very often offers his teachings simply by saying, "When walking, just walk, when hungry, just eat, when sitting, just sit."
This is a beautiful and truly valuable way to train, to make each moment and each activity in that moment, the only thing that is happening. To give our full attention until there is only the 'doingness,' of the moment.
However, as one story says, Soen-Sa-Nim was at the breakfast table one morning, eating his breakfast and reading the paper

when he was seen by some students. They were very upset to see this apparent lack of focus and so they confronted him.

"You know," they said, "you're the master here and you tell us, when walking, just walk, when hungry, just eat, when sitting, just sit. But here you are eating and reading at the same time. How can you explain this?"

He said, "Oh it's very simple, when eating and reading the newspaper, just eat and read the newspaper."

When we don't know for ourselves we need the guidance of rules. Once we know where our real practice is, what need is there for rules?

Life is meditation and meditation is life.

For myself I always found my practice to be life enhancing, something to bring joy to the situation and if not joy, at least the wisdom of knowing.

When we are clear, our life is clear, when we are confused our life is confused.

Dhamma means truth, and truth is always beyond technique.

True masters speak of Love as the answer to all the difficulties of the world, but it is for ardent disciples of Dhamma to hear these words not only with their ears, but with their heart and their whole being, and then apply them to their life.

The moment we defend, support or rationalise violent action, whether through mind, body or speech, we have joined the ranks of the unenlightened and forgotten our heart.

Negotiating our life

At one time somebody arrived at the monastery wanting to speak with my teacher. I arranged the interview and left them in peace.
When the interview was over I met this person again in the kitchen and asked out of politeness if everything was alright. "Yes," he said, "not bad, but this man just does not understand Western psychology."

We fill our life with the confused contents of our mind and then negotiate everything we meet until it fits what we have projected. Rather than being open to the unfolding nature of truth we close ourselves to everything that does not conform to our limited ideas of how things are and should be, and then argue that only we are right and everyone else is wrong. This is not the attitude of the true Dhamma disciple or someone who is willing to learn.
To fully train in Dhamma we must be open to the possibility that everything we have empowered until now is not the truth, but only comfortable ideas.
We build our life around these ideas and then attempt to convince everyone else that we are right and they should listen to us. Security is always in conforming.
The test of our true understanding of life is the amount of happiness, peace and joy we feel in any moment. When the heart is open, suffering is seen only as suffering. Not pleasant to experience to be sure, but not an eternity in hell either.

When we know, we know.
However, when we don't know, we truly don't know!
Building our life around this 'not knowing,' brings us only to the place we find ourselves in right now.

One woman came to me telling me what she thought her daughter should do to be happy. This was a long tirade and included getting married, buying a house and having children. When she had finished speaking I asked her if she was happy.
"Me," she replied, "no, I"m not happy."
"Then what makes you think that you know what other people need to do in order for them to be happy?"

The un-enlightened mind is always in this place. Always ready to teach the other and give a lesson in life, religion and Dhamma.

The mind has three movements that determine the quality of our life : Greed - reaching for an object that it thinks will bring happiness, often manifesting as the thought, 'If only I had that I would be happy.'
Hatred - pushing away an object to which it attributes it's unhappiness, 'If only I didn't have this I would be happy.'
Delusion - that quality of mind that really does believe and empower the other two.
Without awareness these three qualities keep us always facing in the wrong direction and so keep us arguing and rejecting the truth so that we can hold on to our delusions.

There is no difference between the mind of someone from Asia and someone from Europe.
There is no difference between the mind of a man and the mind of a woman. There is no difference between the mind of someone living in India two thousand six hundred years ago and the mind of someone living now in the twenty first century.
Greed is greed, hatred is hatred and delusion is delusion. Mind is mind.

What is different are only the objects of that greed, hatred and delusion, but the movement is always the same.

Perhaps in the time of the Buddha people had greed (desire) for an elephant, whereas now that same desire points towards a sports car. The mental movement is the same, only the object is different.

Western psychology, Eastern psychology, us, them, mine, yours, me, you, just more words illustrating the non-comprehension of mind.
Mind is mind and beings are beings. Without understanding this we will always feel unconnected to the lives of others, and so always struggle with the life we experience.

Before we know Dhammic wisdom as the reality of our life we cannot understand how it can be to live a life without fear or worries. The moment we have it, it is as though we wake up from a deep sleep.

Being the teacher

Many years ago, at the end of another long and intensive meditation retreat with my teacher, I went to his room with my usual end of retreat question. I knelt before him with my hands in anjali, the attitude of respect and gratitude and asked "Bhante, how can I improve my practice?"

He looked at me for a moment before replying, "Ah, Michael, now you must teach."

This was a shock and certainly not the response I had expected.

The idea of teaching others was something that had never entered my mind and I considered myself only to be a disciple of a teacher, never the teacher himself.

It occurred to me that I had misheard the answer, and so I repeated my question.

The response was the same, "Ah, Michael, now you must teach."

With all the humility I could gather, I explained clearly and precisely, exactly why I could not be the teacher.

He listened for a moment and then replied, "I do not ask you for you. I ask you for the people who live on your Island, so that they too might hear the Dhamma"

With such a response how could I refuse?

As with all things from my teacher it was in the service of others.

Thus, slowly and carefully, I began my new life as a Dhamma teacher, although I still insist that I have nothing to teach, and in fact, Dhamma itself cannot be taught. At best we can only share our joy of life, our liberation from fear and our freedom from suffering, but the person called the teacher is nobody.

We can only be the finger that points to the moon but never

the moon itself. In the process of the realisation of pure Dhamma each must make their own effort.

I began to travel, responding to the many generous invitations offered and sharing this beautiful Dhamma as best I could.
The Buddha reminds us that both the teacher and the Dhamma talk should rouse and inspire the heart of the disciple. If I have ever achieved this with my words and my presence, I am happy, if not I ask for your pardon.
My intention has only ever been to share the profound joy and beauty of Dhamma in every moment, so that others may be happy and then share that happiness with all beings.

Don't believe anything.
That which is not the Truth
can only be delusion.

The greatest teachers

It has been a beautiful realisation for me to recognise that my father was actually my hero and first spiritual guide. His influence in my life was something that was always to my benefit.
Growing up in the nineteen sixties, as I did there were many times when my father and I would argue. Perhaps argue is too mild a word. There were ferocious battles of will, each certain that the other was wrong and that we were right. There was never any compromise.
This was a time of great change in society and the generation gap was never wider. New and revolutionary ideas colliding headlong into past conditioning. Long hair, freedom of speech, exotic clothes and music and an interest in new and unusual ways of living. Parents in that time seemed to be old fashioned, firmly established in the past and unwilling to change or even listen to what we had to say. They were most definitely unenlightened.
To think that I could be influenced by one of them seemed to me to be completely out of character.

My father was basically a simple and joyful man who wanted a quiet life. He made no secret of that. He liked things ordered and to run smoothly. He was unpretentious, proud of his working-class roots and had two philosophies that he lived by.

The first was, 'Keep it Simple'.

Although he was a highly intelligent man he knew the value of simplicity in all his dealings and had the ability to strip the situation down to its bare bones. No long intellectual discussions for him, it was always straight to the heart of the matter. He knew what was important and what wasn't and how to cut away the excess.

The second philosophy was, 'Act stupid'.

By this he meant be ready to learn. Don't think you know everything when you don't. Be humble. There is always someone with greater experience and knowledge than you, whatever aspect of life you look at.

Without realising it these two philosophies began to influence me and I see them now as an indication of wisdom.
Of course, when I was young I missed the point, but as the old saying goes, 'When I was eighteen my father knew nothing, but by the time I was twenty five he had learned a lot'.

In my spiritual pursuit, I have been blessed by meeting, working and training with only the best teachers. I feel very privileged to have been in their presence and received instruction from them, but now I see that in principle, their teaching is exactly the same as my father's, 'Keep it simple and act stupid'.

For any living being, the experience of truth is truly a blessing for the whole world. May we all discover its essential simplicity and learn to live in humility.

Here is the Dhamma:
You will not know your delusions
until you awaken from them.

The deepest meditation

During my very first retreat with my teacher thirty years ago, I attained a very deep and profound level of meditation. Actually I didn't attain it - it happened - I was just trying to stay awake!

The retreat had been very difficult for me with lots of pain and discomfort. In those days the monastery was very poor with little or no heating which meant that the Dhamma hall was always like an oven if you sat close to the single gas fire, or like a fridge if you sat anywhere else.

So I was there during the morning session, struggling with pain, sleepiness and the cold continually returning my attention to the breath and sensations in the body when it happened!

Suddenly there was no pain, no sleepiness and no cold. There was only an incredible brightness and lightness of mind, a tremendous feeling of well being and that everything was in balance and harmony. It seemed that my body was not even touching my cushion as I sat there, and that when I walked, as I discovered later, my feet did not touch the floor. This was fantastic!

I sat until the bell was rung and then longer, not wanting to loose this experience until finally a voice inside my head said, "you should go and tell the teacher maybe he can explain this to you."

That was good advice and so I climbed the stairs to my future teachers room.

I gently knocked on the jamb of the door (his door was always open - literally) and he answered, "Come in."

It was in this moment that I realised that I did not know how to approach a Buddhist monk respectfully, and so I said, "Excuse me Bhante, but I don't know how to approach you."

He smiled, gestured with his hand and answered, "Oh, you just walk!"

I knelt down in front of him and described my still on-going meditation experience. He asked some questions which I answered as honestly as possible and he then gave me his interpretation.

"This is jhana," he said, "called piti. It is a very beautiful state of mind, but just watch it because it will pass!"

Just watch it because it will pass.

This is the moment when I realised that I was in front of a true master.

This experience was fantastic. It was wonderful, perhaps even mystical, but it's not IT.

This is not what my practice is about - feeling good in the meditation.

This experience like everything else arises and passes away, to mistake it for something more profound than that is to misunderstand completely the teaching of the Buddha and all the masters ever since.

'Whatever arises passes away and is not what you are.'

Chasing after profound meditation experiences will take us only to more suffering as we continually try to re-create a unique event in time.

One year whist leading our anual series of ten day Vipassana and Loving Kindness retreats in Budh Gaya, a student came to my room with a problem.

Seven years before he had experienced a deep and profound state of meditation and since that moment every time he sat in meditation he would try to re-create the same circumstances to meet the same effect. True suffering.

The Dhamma practice of Vipassana (the way to see things as

they are) is to surrender into this moment of mind, to be with it peacefully and never identify with it as being who and what we are. If it is something pleasant, enjoy it knowing that it will pass. If it is something unpleasant, be with it peacefully, knowing too that it will pass.

According to the Theravada tradition the last great teaching of the Buddha just before he died was, 'Everything that arises passes away and is not what you are. Work hard to understand this truth.'

It is through not understanding the truth of impermanence that we continually empower our suffering by attempting to hold onto those things that by their very nature are always moving away from us. Clouds passing through an empty sky.

This is Dhamma.

Until we truly understand Dhamma
we will compromise everything
to hold on to our delusions.

The deepest Dhamma

This is the most important and profound story that my teacher ever shared with me. It was a daily reflection for so many years and the understanding of this is to see the whole of Dhamma.

At one time an old Brahmin went to speak with the Buddha. "Sir," he said, "Your teaching is so beautiful and profound but as I become older I find it hard to remember so many of the things you have said. Is there a simpler way to share this Dhamma?"
"Old man," the Buddha replied, "there is no need to be concerned, for the whole of my teaching can be expressed in a single sentence. Carry this sentence with you, understand intuitively its essence and be free."
"Please sir," said the Brahmin, "what is this sentence?"
The Buddha answered in this way:

"Nothing whatsoever should be clung to or grasped at as being me or mine."

This perhaps demands a small clarification.

Nothing whatsoever, (nothing at all, not your ideas, your views, your meditation experiences, your religious ideas, your pets, your family, your friends, your body, your mind, nothing, nothing at all!)
should be clung to, (held on to, justified, negotiated with, explained, reasoned, fought for, condemned or approved)
or grasped at, (reached for to bring pleasure in the future, dreams, hopes, aspirations, everything you don't have now that you think will make everything perfect for you)

as being me or mine, (from the delusion of 'self' comes our possessive relationship with life. Organising, controlling, critising and complaining, always building an idea of who and what we are on an insubstantial base).

'Nothing whatsoever should be clung to or grasped at as being me or mine.'

Dhamma is not something to talk about, it's something to do, and the teacher only encourages the disciple to discover the truth for themselves through constant reflection and meditation. This truth is not found in India, China, Tibet or Japan or in any monastery or Dhamma hall, any more than it is found in your own bedroom at home. Our journey is always an internal journey voyaging deeper and deeper to the source of our unhappiness.
So the instruction is always simple: Just make the practice, but don't get lost!
Don't hold on to anything, and don't push anything away. Be with things as they are and allow everything to show you the truth. The true teachers are not outside you, they are arising in every moment. These thoughts, moods, feelings and emotions, arising and passing away. Let their impermanence and their emptiness lead you to true understanding and peace. Reflect all the time:

Nothing whatsoever should be clung to or grasped at as being me or mine.
When we realise the truth of this for ourselves, not as an intellectual idea, something to be promoted and explained, but as an intuitive realisation, we will know life as it really is and not be lost in the delusion of mind manifesting as 'I, me, mine and my,' and so creating the world of 'me,' and 'the

other,' 'us,' and 'them.'

Our work of Loving Awareness is often called 'the way of letting go,' and ultimately our journey is always an unlearning process. To let go, and let go, and let go, until there is nothing left to let go of. To become more and more silent.
In the Theravada tradition of Buddhism this is called the Vishudhimagga - the path of Purification.
To purify the mind by letting go of the delusions that cover our inherent wisdom.
We can talk and argue about our spiritual understanding, but the true test of our Dhamma is found in the quality of our life - how we live and how we love, and how much idea of 'self,' we still carry.

The Buddha did not get enlightenment - he realised it! It was a quality he had carried with him always. This same potential is the sleeping giant within you.

Reflect: Nothing whatsoever should be clung to or grasped at as being me or mine, - and watch your suffering ebb away.

The Dhamma life is not a fantasy life, but it can stay that way without the effort required to make it real. The feelings of love and compassion come to nothing if we do not make the effort to bring them to reality, to bring them into our daily life.

Feeding the mind

Although Dhamma is always very simple, it is rarely very easy to apply, even when we are able to see the mechanics of our mind, of our life and of our suffering.

Life as we usually experience it is a series of habits, recurring mind states empowered through unawareness, moment after moment. The more often we empower them the more we cultivate the habit of them and so the more often they return. Our life becomes cyclic as we find ourselves in the same kinds of situations over and over again, reacting in the same way over and over again, and always experiencing the same outcome, over and over again. How could it be different?

The International Meditation Centre, just outside Budh Gaya, in northern India, is the place where we would conduct our annual series of ten day highly intensive Vipassana meditation retreats, from November to February each year.

These were always well attended and the students who came to sit with us had many opportunities to observe their own habits of mind, both in the sitting meditation practice and in their limited daily activity.

We would begin our day at five o'clock in the morning with sitting meditation and so breakfast, two hours later, was always welcome.

Life on retreat is deliberately kept as simple as possible, principally to give space to the mind, and so breakfast was always the same meal consisting of porridge, a small banana and two cookies.

However, for whatever reason, the cookies were not popular with the students and so they would keep them to one side and then when they had finished eating, take them out of the dining room to feed to the dogs.

The International Meditation Centre had three dogs that would roam about the property freely all day, but every morning at breakfast time they would be waiting outside the dining room to be fed with cookies. The more they were fed, the more they came back. Every day was the same, no surprises and no changes. The dogs would appear, wag their tails, open their mouths and they would be fed. The relationship between the two forces never deviated. The dogs arrived and they were fed.

The mind is exactly the same. The more we feed it the more it returns - more dogs waiting for cookies. To change this habit we don't have to kill or destroy the dogs, of course not, we only have to stop feeding them. Only in this way will they stop coming every day for food.

Dhamma is always very simple, though rarely very easy, but changing our life is mostly about remembering to be different. To stop feeding the habits of our mind and so be free.

Without wisdom there is only intelligence,
without love there is only fear.

Self without love

Human beings are a pretty strange and complicated life-force and although the potential for complete liberation is present in every moment, mostly we take the other route, that of suffering.

One of the most common expressions of this suffering in the West is the bizzare pre-occupation with low self esteem. How did we arrive in this place where we continually think that we are no good, or at least not good enough, and then so often feel intimidated and threatened by everything around us?

Of course the media exploits this situation endlessly by reminding us that what we feel is actually the truth and without the latest perfume, shampoo, car, magazine, etc, we will never be enough in the eyes of others.

To fall into this trap is real suffering, for when will we ever be good enough? How many times will we need to be told that we are loved before we feel worthy of that love? If one hundred people tell you that you are a wonderful human being, and one person tells you that you are no good, who do you believe, the one or the hundred?

Low self esteem is only another conditioned suffering in our life, the foundation of it is an illusion established naturally in delusion, and so has no value.

I have heard that when the Dalai Lama was asked what Tibetan people do about low self esteem he replied, "Do about what???"

It is a quality of being that does not exist for them.

At one time, whilst living with my teacher in his monastery, I bumped into the Dhamma of low self esteem.

After our early morning meditation I had the privilige (truly I felt like this) to prepare his breakfast in the kitchen.

Sometime later he would arrive and I would smile and offer a polite and friendly greeting. "Good morning Bhante, did you sleep well?" His reply was always a grunt!

I persisted, day after day to enquire after him, his health and his quality of sleep until one day he actually spoke to me.

"You British," he said, "you're so polite always saying hello and asking after the other person. In Burma we make the assumption that we are always pleased to see each other and so find no need to continually speak in this way!"

'We make the assumption that we are always pleased to see each other,' how beautiful is this?

Which one of us highly programmed and conditioned westerners would dare to make an assumption like that, that our presence in any situation needs no qualification? To be there is enough.

I realise now of course, that my questions were only subtle attempts for him to notice me (which he always did of course) but more, to be validated. His teaching ultimately was 'put this idea down, it will never lead you to peace and never bring happiness. You're fine as you are, no need to feel less than that.'

In every situation the response to our difficulties has to be love, first for ourselves and then for the other. Only when we love ourselves will we be able to truly love the other, and only when we love ourselves will we be able to allow the other to love us. Dhamma is everywhere and our liberation is always right in front of us in every moment.

I trained with this man as a monk and a layman for thirty years, he only ever showed me love, compassion and kindness. He always offered the gift of truth, but in every moment it was for me to accept it or not. This is the way of Dhamma.

Enlightenment is not personal.
When you do the practice in the right way,
that's what happens.

Making the practice

Many years ago whilst on yet another intensive ten day Vipassana and Loving Kindness retreat at my teachers monastery, myself and the small group I was part of were meditating in the Dhamma hall. My teacher was in front of us and when the meditation ended, he did not move. This could only mean one thing, he was going to present a Dhamma talk. This was always a source of joy to me, to listen to his words, to take them inside and reflect upon what he had said. The Buddha himself, according to Theravada tradition, has said that to hear the Dhamma is one of the thirty eight blessings in life (The Mangala Sutta), and certainly this was always my experience.

I could and did, meditate at home three times a day, but to hear the words of Dhamma from him was always something exceptional and to be with a true master, having already been accepted as a disciple, can only ever be experienced as an honour and a privilige.

However, the only role of the master is to present Dhamma and not allow the disciple to be fooled by anything - especially by themselves.

As we were sitting quietly my teacher looked at me and spoke.

"Michael, what do you understand by the word, ardent?"

Ardent is a word found many times in the suttas to describe the necessary attitude of the true disciple.

I felt pleased and honoured that in front of the others he would choose me to define this important word and so I gave the standard definition.

"Bhante, ardent means to be determined, to be focused on practice, to be disciplined and to make liberation our goal."

"Yes," he replied, "so why are you sitting with your watch in front of you?"

He got me!

I wasn't sitting for enlightenment, liberation or Nibbana, I was sitting for an hour. It's not the same thing!
Every time I would enter the Dhamma hall I would take off my wristwatch and gently place it in front of me. Then I would time the meditation. One hour, in those days, and not a second more. If someone didn't ring the bell at the right moment a lot of coughing and throat clearing would follow!
It may be obvious that from that moment I never brought my watch into the Dhamma hall again, and always surrendered completely to the meditation.

The gift of the master is the training given to their disciples. There was no intention in my teachers mind to embarrass or humiliate me, such a thought would not occur to him, only to show directly that beyond the physicality of my sitting posture, something was missing.
Dividing our life into time slots is common and can be useful in daily life, but Dhamma demands much more than that. Dhamma demands total immersion whether we are sitting, standing, walking or lying down.
Dhamma demands that we are determined, focused on our practice, disciplined and that we make liberation our goal.
Dhamma demands that we are ardent.

Behind all our fears,
anxieties and negotiations with life
lies the true loving heart of liberation.
Freedom is not something to get,
it is something to realise.

Cleaning the pool

One day, during my time as a monk with my teacher, I was asked to clean the small pool in the garden. As always, I was very happy to assist my teacher in any way and this day as the sun was shining it seemed like a good opportunity to be outside for a time.

I began by gently catching the many small fish that lived there and re-housing them temporarily in a bucket of water. Next was the situation with the frogs - wonderful creatures for me, and having put them to one side I began to clean the pool. Not difficult and so it didn't take too long. The sun was shining, the birds were singing and I was happily focused in my small work.

Soon I had replaced the water and gently again put the fishes back one by one. But now something happened.

As I sat there with my shaven head and monks robes watching these small creatures finding once more their freedom I had a tremendous insight - the insight of 'Oneness,' the interconnectedness of all life.

This intuitive understanding brought with it an immense sense of peace and completeness and I sat gazing into the water watching these small creatures, now no longer beings outside and separate from me.

My teacher arrived and saw me sitting quite still just looking into the water.

"Paññadipa (my monks name) what are you doing? You don't have to sit there all afternoon." he said.

"Yes Bhante, I know, but I have just understood the reality of oneness. There is no separation between me, these fish and everything else that exists." I replied.

He looked at me for a moment, smiled and went back inside.

Such an obvious truth needs no comment and it had only taken ten years of his teaching for this truth to finally arise in me. When the heart is truly open everything is seen to be the way it is, and spontaneously has equal value. The intellectual discriminating mind can always find space to explain and justify the cruelty and killing of every life form, from the biggest mamals to the smallest insects, and everything in between.

Interconnectedness is the intuitive manifestation of unconditional and limitless love and the understanding of the inherent 'oneness' of all things.

One Zen master was asked what it was like when he became enlightened. He replied, "Everyone I met had my face."
In other words, I saw me in everyone, and everyone in me.
Beautiful!

This understanding stays with me always and here in our forest, our cats, the wild pigs and deer, the mosquitos and every other insect, all have my face.
This life is blessed.

> All beings fear pain and death.
> Remembering that we are one of them,
> we will neither hurt nor kill.
> Dhammapada Verse: 129

Only when we are able to live in harmony with our own reality will we be able to live in harmony with the reality of others, and so bring something truly beneficial to the world.

The most important thing

In my young life I spent seven years practicing alone. I had already trained for some time in Zen, both the Rinzai and Soto styles but because of geography (I had returned home to the Isle of Man) there was no group and certainly no teacher to support me.
So I made my practice every day, quietly and alone. It was not always easy but I had three small books that were my constant inspiration. They were all by the same author, a Sri Lankan Buddhist monk named Hamalawa Saddhatissa. Immediately upon finishing the first I would begin the second, then having finished that, the third and then back to the first again. Even though we had never met, I considered Bhante Saddhatissa to be my first Theravada teacher.

Many years later and having been accepted as a disciple and already instructed to teach on the Isle of Man, I invited my now teacher, Sayadaw Rewata Dhamma, to visit us and lead another retreat for our group there.
He asked me if he could bring a friend with him, I immediately said yes and asked who the friend was.
"It's Hamalawa Saddhatissa," he replied, "do you know him?"

During the retreat I was with my two great teachers when Sayadaw Rewata Dhamma told Bhante Saddhatissa that I would be taking full ordination as a Buddhist monk in the next year.
"When you are in robes," he said, "I will come to see you."
This was a very nice thing to say, but in truth I didn't believe it for a moment. I felt it was simple friendliness and politeness from such a lovely man.

One morning, some days after my ordination, I was in my room meditating when my teacher arrived, "Paññadipa," he said, "Venerable Saddhatissa is downstairs waiting to see you."
I could hardly believe it. This great man had travelled all this way to see me. I arranged my robes and went downstairs to meet him.
Venerable Saddhatissa was sitting in an armchair in the anteroom of the monastery and so I immediately knelt in front of him, bowed three times and presented anjali (hands held in front in an attitude of prayer).
"Bhante," I began, "thank you so much for coming. It is a pleasure and a privilige to see you here."
"Yes, yes, yes," he said gently touching my arm, "now tell me, are you getting enough to eat?"

Dhamma training is the way to be free, to live with love and be aware. To find happiness for ourselves so that we can share that happiness with all beings. The greatest teachers manifest this happiness and love in their relationship with their students.
The fundamental things are the ones we have to address. Are you comfortable, are you warm, do you have enough to eat? The Buddha himself discovered that we have to be strong and healthy to make the practice and so the basic requirements for life are the primary concern.
The real masters are like loving fathers, hard when they need to be, but always loving. Their advice is pure Dhamma. Take care of you, so that you can take care of others. When you have energy you will share that. When you are tired you will share that. Be something of value in the world.

There are no secrets in Dhamma. Truth is truth, love is love, wisdom is wisdom and these qualities always manifest in the simple and spontaneous acts of caring and kindness.

(Hamalawa Saddhatissa 1914 - 1990)

Meditation is the most important gift
we can give ourselves in this life.

The power of Love

One day my teacher told me of an incident that had happened in the monastery. An English woman, a friend of his, had arrived and was immediately angry with him, standing in front of him shouting and waving her arms. I was shocked to hear this, for in my mind I could not understand how anyone could be angry at this beautiful, smiling, brown skinned man, so I asked the question, "Bhante, what did you do?"
"Oh," he said, "I just waited for the anger to pass, then my friend was back."
This is the power of love.

Without understanding, perhaps this story shows that when we are weak we will accept the anger and abuse from others? With true understanding we will see that it is the absolute power of love that allows us to be in difficult situations in life and not take them personally and equally importantly, not be drawn into the madness of the world and react, like with like. When there is no wisdom and no love this is how the world manifests. Anger leading to more anger, fighting leading to more fighting, killing leading to more killing.

> Hatred is never overcome by more hatred.
> Only love overcomes hatred,
> This is an eternal law.
> Dhammapada: verse 5

It is only when we are out of balance that we allow ourselves to be abused and drawn into conflict. Choosing, taking sides, arguing who is right and who is wrong, always seeking blame and humiliation of the other.
Love exists beyond this level of mind and is the only true and

real balance in our life.
It is love that will bring peace to ourselves and the world, but this practice of Loving Kindness (Metta Bhavana) is rarely fully understood.
People have told me that their style of Loving Kindness is different from mine and that they take all the people that they don't like and wrap them in pink fluffy clouds, "but you know," they say, "they're still as horrible as ever!"

Here is the truth we must understand: We don't practice Loving Kindness to change the other. We practice Loving Kindness so that we can be with the other - however they are! This is our strength, not to continually insist that the world and everything in it is always the way we think it should be so that we can be happy. Vipassana and Loving Kindness is a very mature way of life and living, it says 'I accept you as you are and make no demands that you should be different so that I can be happy.'

Love is the real and beautiful power in our life.
It is never weak and never subservient. It manifests in every moment as complete and unconditional acceptance of the universe exactly as it is in this moment. Things are like this, that is the reality of this moment, now, what is our place in this?
With awareness we see, with love we accept, with wisdom we respond.
This is the whole of the Dhamma.

However, introducing Love into your life will bring some difficulties as many students new to Dhamma practice discover.

Many years ago I was invited to present a seven day course in France. I was happy to do this and met very lovely people there, including one young French woman who impressed me somewhat with her conduct.

Two months later I was invited back to teach the same group again.

However, even before the course began this young woman asked for a private interview with me. I naturally said yes and she arrived with the translator and was immediately angry with me, telling me I should not travel around the world encouraging people to live with love. It just brings more and more difficulties and more and more frustration. Her life had been turned upside down and now she really struggled.

In truth I have no recollection of this interview and this story was told to me by the young woman involved, so I asked her, "What did I say?"

"Oh," she said, "you just smiled and told me I needed more loving kindness."

Fourteen years after these first two meetings, this young woman and I married and now live lovingly in our forest in France.

The Dhamma is always simple.
Make your practice with humility.
Don't pretend to be something that you are not,
you will always show yourself,
and most importantly,
live with love and be aware.

Honesty in practice

For many years during my training as a lay Buddhist I meditated for two and a half hours a day. I would get up at five o'clock in the morning to meditate before going to work. At work during my lunch break, I would discretely meditate again for half an hour and then at home in the evening I would sit for another hour. It was a strong practice for me and I was happy to do it, but it was exhausting. Beginning and ending each day in this way often took it's toll.

One evening I began my final meditation before going to bed and quickly started to fall asleep. I shook myself and continued with my practice. Once more I began to slip into sleep. This happened many times until finally I looked at the statue of the Buddha that my teacher had given me, put my hands together in anjali and apologised.

"I'm so sorry," I said, "but I can't continue, I'm just too tired." Then it hit me!

What am I doing, apologising to a statue? This is complete nonsense.

If I truly am too tired to meditate that's OK, no dishonour in that. If I'm just making an excuse not to finish my sitting time, that is something I can reflect upon, but in any case I am responsible for my practice and my life, not someone or something outside me.

Self responsibility is something very important in Dhamma training. Without understanding it properly we are always able to make excuses and blame others for our conduct, but the truth shows us something different.

The words and actions that we cast into the world comes from ourselves and although we are always responding and reacting to the external conditions, ultimately it is us who acts or not. It is us who speaks or not.

The foundation of Dhamma training is awareness and love. It is the first and last teaching, the simplest and the most profound, and it's place in our life is essential.

With awareness we are able to see the reality of the moment. With love we are able to accept that reality peacefully. With wisdom we can respond.

Making excuses may make us feel better, but if we are honest there is no reason to excuse anything. When we have integrity and are clear in our determination to be liberated from our suffering, we will always accept the reality of the moment, that whatever the provocation, whatever the difficulty, it is ourselves that determine our response. Accepting the reality of self responsibility is the mark of wisdom and the mark of the true disciple.

The most practical thing we can do for ourselves
is live a life established in love and awareness,
then we will be happy
and share that happiness with all beings.

Love me like you love your cat

Almost thirty years ago I was a young married man living on the Isle of Man in a small terraced house. Our neighbours were also a young married couple and the wife, Lucie was heavily pregnant. Her husband, Peter had an old car that was not always reliable and so I made an offer to them. If Lucie goes into labour and the car won't start, come and get me. No matter what time of day or night I will make myself available for you and drive you to the hospital. Some days later, at about two thirty in the morning, I was awoken by someone rattling the letter box. It was persistent and sounded urgent. My only thought was, "Lucie's in labour and the car won't start." I quickly grabbed some clothes and stumbled down the stairs still half asleep, shouting "coming, coming!" I opened the front door but saw no-one. The only creature in sight was our cat Bimbo (named after my fathers favourite Jim Reeves song), looking up at me as if to say, "about time, I've been rattling this letterbox for ages!" He walked past me into the house without a second glance and as I watched him disappear into the lounge, my only thought was, 'that was really clever. Well done Bimbo!'

Dhamma is everywhere and the teachers of Dhamma are gifts in our life.
If you are a cat owner you have one of the greatest teachers in the world in front of you. Look at your relationship with your cat. Look what it can do without you becoming upset or even annoyed. Our relationship with our cat is based in an unconditional acceptance of everything they do. If our cat takes the best seat in the house we don't mind. If our cat wants to go out it will sit by the door until we get up and open it. If our cat wants a caress or food, we give that. Our relationship

to our cat is one of almost perfect loving kindness. This of course, applies to all the animals we love. So here is the teaching: Reflect upon this relationship and try to emulate the same unconditional acceptance for all beings. When you radiate these same feelings for everyone and everything in the world, you will not suffer. Not only that, your presence in the world will bring benefit to all the different beings you come into contact with. Love is not about liking something, it is about accepting that thing as it is, and even if humans are often much more difficult to accept than animals, our practice is here and opportunities are always in front of us.

Our spiritual life is our worldly life, and our worldly life is our spiritual life.
We do not need to be meditating in a monastery or a cave in the Himalayas to train, we need only to raise the intention to change how we live.
In this respect, the teaching is always around us.

Dhamma Bum

For many years I travelled intensively teaching, sharing Dhamma wherever I was invited. I had almost everything I owned in my back-pack and earned the somewhat affectionate, and for me quite romantic name, of 'Dhamma Bum.' I lived then, as now, from the kindness of others who saw the value in generosity and supporting an earnest disciple of Dhamma. This life suited me well, inspired as I was by the Buddha, Gandhi and David Carradine as Kwai Chang Caine, just a few of my Dhamma heros. I would sleep on the floor in people's houses if no bed was available and even outside when the weather was warm enough. Each winter I would arrive in Budh Gaya, my spiritual home, to lead three months of intensive Vipassana meditation retreats at the International Meditation Centre. It was my blessed life and a great, great training in a slightly ascetic manner. In the spring of 1998 I arrived in Israel. Invited by my closest friend I spent the summer there teaching in the garden of the house where I stayed and giving open Dhamma talks in the park in Tel Aviv on Friday afternoons. I also taught two big retreats in Jerusalem and Tel Aviv as well as courses on two kibbutz. Each time and in every moment I met only kindness and friendliness. The Sangha was large and we worked together well, looking at many aspects of Dhamma study. I continually encouraged them to practice and to work hard for their own liberation. Meditate, meditate, meditate. Let go, let go, let go. Awareness and love. At the end of the summer I left and returned to the U.K. without any firm idea of ever returning to Israel. This was the time when I saw the great disservice I was giving to others.

During my training, and in fact until the day he died, my teacher was always there for me. Even if he was travelling to teach in another country, his date of return was known and whatever difficulty I had, I could always wait, knowing that he would be available for me sooner or later. At the end of my stay in Israel, for the first time in my life I understood the responsibility of the teacher. If I encourage students to turn to Dhamma, I must be available for them when they meet some difficulty. If not it can be as though I cast them off in a boat smiling and waving at them saying, 'have a nice time, everything will be fine,' but giving them no-one to turn to if a storm breaks. The foundation of Dhamma is love, and love means to take care of those we are connected to. Teachers and students, masters and disciples, this is perhaps the closest of all relationships. To open yourself completely to another and ask, "Please show me the way - even if I have so many things, I still don't know how to be completely happy," The master gives the teaching, the disciple applies it. Slowly, slowly understanding arises and the relationship grows and evolves. But this takes two people committed to serving each other. One without the other always leaves a space that must be filled. Of course, in the end, it is this mind and the life it projects that is the teacher, but to have the presence of a Dhamma friend, one who has already walked this path, to remind us of this is invaluable.

Every day, in one way or another, I put my hands together in anjali to say 'thank you' to my ordinary but wonderful life for everything it has given and shown me. Dhamma understanding is always right in front of us - no need to look further.

The future is the great unknown, but our relationship to it is determined by our understanding and our wisdom in this moment.
How can we be afraid of that which does not yet exist?
Only through delusion.
How can we be free?
Only through wisdom.
Live with love and be aware - the whole of the Dhamma and complete liberation is here.

Influencing others

Some years ago whilst waiting for my flight at Toulouse airport, I saw four Buddhist monks in the departure lounge. As is my custom I approached them to see if I could offer anything, a cup of tea for example. They were sitting opposite each other and so I leaned in, offered anjali and asked if I could be of service. One of the young monks looked at me and said, "Hello Michael." I was surprised that he knew my name and so asked if we knew each other. "Oh yes," he said, "in fact it's because of you that I am now a monk!"

No matter how we live or what we do we cannot help but have an effect in the universe that we are part of. We speak, we smile, we scowl, we laugh, always influencing the events and beings around us. This young Buddhist monk reminded me that he had sat two meditation retreats with me in India some years before and something about my presentation of Dhamma had touched his heart and his journey began. When we live without the desire to influence or persuade others as to how they should be, we show something beautiful - we show Dhamma. A young woman in my room one time on retreat told me that she had fallen in love with me. This happens occasionally and as always, compassion and integrity are the qualities needed, for ourselves, for the other and for the reputation of Dhamma. When someone makes themselves vulnerable in front of us it is our responsibility to take care of them, not exploit the situation. When I responded to her words she continued, "How could I not be in love with someone who listens to all the terrible things I say about myself, but never judges?" This is how Dhamma manifests. Not by judging or telling others how they should be, what they should wear or how they should think, but being peacefully with the moment as it is, and then responding wisely. Love is always an expression of wisdom. I saw this with my teacher always, and it was inspiring to me, to put down the fears that would show themselves in subtle ways of control, and be free. The true master does not have a view as to how others should be in their life. They know that they can only be responsible for themselves. Dhamma is always given without conditions. It is the greatest thing that we can meet in our life and following this Dhamma path can take us only to peace. This world does not need greater weapons technology. This world does not need clever politicians and religious leaders encouraging others to kill. This world needs love, and that love is found in Dhamma.

The words of the master are always given freely for the disciple to accept or reject, as they like. We are all responsible for ourselves in every moment, and so the Dhamma emanating from the master tells us to choose wisely and listen to our heart.

There are no rules to take us to enlightenment,
only the foundations of Awareness and Love.

Don't wash the dishes

Some years ago I had a student who was a mature woman, divorced and sharing her house with her two adult sons. All three were working and so an agreement was reached. The mother would prepare, cook and serve the evening meal, and the sons would clear the table and wash the dishes afterwards. This arrangement worked well until the mother began to train with me and learn the two meditations of awareness and love. After some time she began to notice that when she had prepared, cooked and served the evening meal, the sons would clear the table but leave the dishes piled up in the sink unwashed. If she began to complain about this the sons would listen for a moment and then say, almost in unison, "Ah, you're getting angry, you need to meditate!" She would suddenly stop and think, 'Yes, I am getting angry, I do need to meditate.' She would go to her cushion, meditate and then come back and wash the dishes. Naturally she became tired of this and asked me what she could do. I told her simply, 'don't be a victim to your sons manipulation, and definitely don't wash the dishes!'

Before wisdom arises there is often a misunderstanding of what it means to be a student of Dhamma. It does not mean that simply because you have begun a meditation practice, you should never be angry again or that you should never stand up for yourself. Being a student of Dhamma means that we are training ourselves in the disciplines of awareness and love. Awareness to see things as they really are, and love to accept them as they really are, and as they manifest in this moment. The arising wisdom from this training will allow us to respond to life in a way that recognises the equal validity of ourselves and the other in every moment and in every situation. This is very important! You have the same right to happiness as every one else, not more, but never less! A student of mine in France asked me, "If I practice Loving Kindness for others, won't they just take advantage of me?" I replied, "If that really happens, whatever you think you're doing, you are not practising loving kindness."

The first person we have to love is ourselves, and love is never weak. It is never aggressive or arrogant, but it is always strong, and in the end it is the only thing that will serve us in difficult moments. Love itself has the quality of honesty and simplicity and so there is never the need to explain or justify your position. From love and wisdom, we can say what we need to say, and then give the space to others to decide what they want to do in this situation. The moment we begin to explain, justify and defend our anger or unhappy feeling, we are lost. If we have an agreement with others, we have the right to expect that the agreement will be upheld, whether we are meditators or not.

My student was able to do this by speaking quietly and directly to her sons, where she could say, "We have an agreement, I will cook the dinner and you will wash the dishes. If you don't want to wash the dishes, I won't cook for you. This is simple and clear. Now you must decide for yourselves what you want to do." This is the teaching. You are not here to be the victim of anyone, and taking that position will not ultimately help you or the other person.

Live with love and be aware. Be happy in your life by loving yourself and not falling victim to the manipulations of others. Bring something beautiful to the world - a brave, clear you!

The biggest obstacle to the teacher is the mind of the student. The biggest obstacle to the student is also the mind of the student.

To meet the truth we must let go of our preconceived ideas as to what the truth really is.

We must be empty of personal views and opinions and be ready to receive the beautiful ordinariness of reality.

Using the words

At one time I was teaching at a local group and I arrived early. I parked my car next to the most beautiful car I have ever seen. Now, I have no interest what-so-ever in cars, but this was special. The ascetics were incredible. It was a bottle green Jaguar, low, sleek and smooth. The interior was clean with deep plush seats and a polished wooden dashboard. It was like looking at a beautiful sunrise. I had no desire to own it, but I could certainly appreciate it's inherent beauty. I went in to the Dhamma hall to meet the only person there, a woman whom I had met two or three times previously. "Is that your car outside?" I asked. "Yes," she replied, "but I'm not attached!"

There is a way to speak that people often use to convey the sentiment that they know Dhamma. There is a jargon and a style that covers their true non-understanding, and that they can talk about attachment, kamma, suffering and the rest as though they have already transcended. As though they know. The truth is however, that only people who don't know speak in this way, those who carry Dhamma in their hearts speak naturally and honestly about life, never making a show.

> Those who speak do not know.
> Those who know do not speak.
>
> Tao te Ching verse 128

It is true that attachment is the cause of our suffering because in the end, whatever we are attached to will hurt us. It is inevitable and the proof of this, as with everything that is Dhammic, is found in our ordinary daily life. Reflect, why do you suffer? The answer is always simple, it is because in this moment you are attached to an idea of how things should be. The reality does not meet your idea and so suffering arrives. Subtle or gross it is always like this. However, without fully understanding the words of the teacher we think that we are being told that we shouldn't have any attachments, but this is not the truth. The master tells us that whatever we are attached to will hurt us - that's all! How we move with this is in our life is for us to discover for ourselves. Attachment is subtle and when we are attached to even one thing, the whole universe of attachment is in front of us. One student of mine told me once that she had no attachments at all, except for her own bed at night. It doesn't seem to be very much, but the attachment to this one simple thing opens the door for everything else. From one attachment the whole universe of attachments arises. So our way is always to be honest and recognise that attachment is just attachment, no need to pretend it's not there. It's not wrong to be attached, it just brings a consequence, that's all.

Playing the Dhamma game in front of others has no value at all, especially in front of the teacher, and liberation will come when we realise that our suffering and unhappiness has a cause, and that we can do something about it. So, the next time you are unhappy, find a quite place alone and ask yourself, 'In this moment, what is it that I am attached to?' The answer will always be the same, 'I am attached to the idea that this moment should be different from the way it is!' Once we accept the reality of this moment and surrender into it, there is no space for suffering to arise.

Enjoy what can be enjoyed and let go. Endure what has to be endured, and let go. This is true liberation.

The best time to practice love and awareness
is now - right now in this moment
with these very conditions.
Nothing is missing and here exists the perfect opportunity
for liberation.

Being enlightened

On one occasion in Budh Gaya, India, I was eating in a small cafe when two young women who had attended one of my introductory courses of Vipassana and Loving Kindness meditation at the Lotus Tank, arrived and asked if they could join me. We sat together and talked in a friendly manner. After some time they looked at each other, smiled and then turned to me to tell me something. "We think that you are enlightened," they said. I was surprised to hear such a thing and so patiently and lovingly began to explain exactly why and how I was not enlightened. They listened expressionless until I had finished, glanced and smiled at each other again and said, "That's exactly what an enlightened being would say!"

Dhamma is simple. Live with love and be aware. It is only the mind that complicates this teaching and says that it is not enough. The mind, invested as it is in fascination and distraction from simply being, always seeks something outside the reality of the moment. One time in Pokara, Nepal, I heard a group of westerners talking about and comparing sunsets. In Pokara of course the sun sets behind the Himalayas casting a beautiful red glow on the mountains before it disappears completely. The conversation was, 'which is better, the sunset here or in the Alps?' This is called, missing the moment, missing that which is right in front of us. The mind that always judges, compares and carries the past cannot be free. It cannot see something purely for what it is and so must create a comparison, a framework for judgement. According to Theravada tradition the Buddha has told us that it is impossible to recognise enlightenment in another until we too are enlightened. This seems realistic to me as it applies to all other areas of life. To be truly able to see, beyond a superficial value, a quality in another being we too must have that quality, if not we simply follow the mind, comparing and making assumptions. How will we recognise the subtleties and nuances of the French language unless we speak French ourselves? Often, to bring something exciting or exotic to our life, we look for something special in our spiritual practice. A secret meditation only whispered to special disciples, and an enlightened teacher. But take care with this. Enlightenment is rare, and beware of anyone who tells you that they have it! It can be an easy vehicle for exploitation. On one occasion in Budh Gaya a man applied for a place at one of our meditation retreats. He was talking to my retreat manager, and when the negotiations were completed, he began to walk away. Suddenly he stopped, turned around and asked a question, "Is Michael enlightened?" "Oh," said my manager, "I don't think he's very interested in that." "Then I can't sit with him," said the man, and walked away. Enlightened teachers are not the point. Love and awareness is the point. The practice and efforts of others is not the point, only our own dedication to Dhamma is the point. The enlightenment of others, real or imagined is not the point, only our own understanding of Dhamma as we meet it moment after moment has real value in our life.

When the heart is open, the face smiles.

What is enough?

At one time a student of mine was also a student of psychology, taking a degree course in this subject. She had to write an essay entitled 'A satisfactory relationship.' She asked me what would be the Dhamma perspective on this subject, I answered simply, "Don't accept satisfactory."

When we aspire to excellence in our spiritual practice, everything is possible. If not, we stand still and accept that which is only satisfactory. Our effort falls away and we stay in one place, talking about Dhamma and enlightenment as though we know what they are, but never moving forward. Being comfortable in our practice, but still asleep. This easy, satisfactory sentiment is often the understanding of the Buddha's great teaching of the eightfold path, before we realise it's true depth and profundity.

Traditionally, the teaching of the Buddha is known as the Middle Way, the way between extremes. However, this is not really accurate for it implies only a life of moderation - a little bit of this and a little bit of that. Not completely angry, only irritated, not completely happy, only pleased. Not completely wise, only intelligent.

The Middle Way of the Buddha is a gift to the world, for it shows the path to the complete realisation of the Truth and so the way to complete peace. This Middle Way is not a way between extremes, but the way beyond extremes. It is the transcendent way.

The understanding of this path is very important if we want to go beyond religion, and blind faith, personal views and opinions.

Talking about it won't help much, but applying it to our moment to moment life will change everything. The transcendent path that the Buddha revealed to his disciples at the Isipatana deer sanctuary is the way to no longer be a prisoner of the mind, which is the sole cause of our suffering and unhappiness.

Through the practice of Vipassana meditation we can see the very nature of this mind, and by seeing, be free from it's influence. By letting go of our attachment to the mind as being who and what we are, we can enjoy it when it presents something pleasant, and not suffer when it changes. But also, we can be with this mind peacefully when it presents something unpleasant, knowing intuitively, that it too will pass. Impermanence is the nature of all things. To harmonise and flow with this impermanence is to be one with the Truth itself, and is the nature of enlightenment.

Each life deserves to be more than satisfactory, and it can be when we apply ourselves to excellence in every moment and every situation.

If we don't aspire to complete illumination how will our suffering ever end?

The Way of Dhamma is to stay in balance and allow the world to be as it is, letting go of all judgement and recrimination and to transcend the limitations of fear.
Beings are the way they are, that's their choice, but you are the way you are, and that's your choice!
So how are you choosing to be today?

The nature of fear

One time on retreat in India a woman came to me to tell me of her dream the night before. In her dream, she arrived in my room with her hand clenched into a fist. Inside this fist was something frightening. She didn't know what it was, but she was afraid to open her hand to see. I encouraged her to open her hand and when she finally did, it was empty, there was nothing there. This was her dream and she asked my to explain it's meaning. For me it was very clear. This is the nature of fear, we create something in the mind and hold onto it, but when we look, it's actually empty.

Our common human goal is happiness and our common human condition is fear. Fear is the obstacle in every moment to our happiness and our complete illumination. It is fear that holds us in a job or a relationship or a situation that we don't like or enjoy, and it is this fear that society continually caresses. Have insurance, don't get wrinkles, don't get old, don't take a chance! The media report fear, always because when people are afraid they can be controlled, and of course, fear sells products. Fear is a powerful tool that can be used in the manipulation of others. From the Dhammic perspective however, fear has no value, and our ultimate goal of enlightenment is outside it's influence and consequently outside it's power to control. When you have no fear you are free from the possibility of all manipulation and this is the true liberation. Our loving practice therefore is to let go of the fear and be free, little by little, and experience our life opening like a flower. Living peacefully and harmoniously with the things that we don't like and then responding wisely to each moment. So here is the secret of fear, it's empty. No matter how much you can explain it or justify it, it's empty and, as with everything else that begins with mind, it only has the power that you give it. What is it that you are afraid of? Reflect honestly, it's a big question, and it's through the unawareness of the power of this fear that keeps you and holds you in many situations that are uncomfortable. In our culture we say quite confidently that we are afraid of the unknown, but I ask you, if it's unknown how can we be afraid of it? It's a way to speak, but it's not the truth. We are afraid of loosing the known, that which is familiar and comfortable - even if, paradoxically, we don't like it. We keep our suffering because we hold onto our fear. Fear is the key that locks the cell door, and the intellect is the part that justifies it. Talk to your parents and your friends and they will explain quite clearly why it's important to have fear. Speak to the Dhamma masters, what will they say? Let go, let go, let go. Enlightenment is called waking up. When we are asleep our dream is real. When we are awake we can see it for what it truly is.

Now is the time to open your hand and see the reality. Now is the time to be free.

The master lives quietly and alone, even in the midst of others.
For him (or her) there is only Dhamma, manifesting in each moment and in all things.
There is nothing to say, nothing to do, nothing to get and nothing to become.
There is only the reality of oneness, the connectedness with life itself.

Communicating Dhamma

For many years I worked in a factory. It was, in the end, a good place to train myself, to watch the mind and it's endless resentment and complaining. It was during my time there that I truly understood one of the most important lessons in Dhamma. One day I received a hand written note from another department with instructions about a certain piece of work that need to be completed. However, the writing on this note was illegible! I showed it to my colleagues but none of us could decipher it. The only thing that I could do was to cross the whole factory, find the person who wrote it and ask what it meant. This is what I did, and the insight from this particular moment, of standing with an illegible note in my hand in front of the person who had written it, has stayed with me forever and shaped a huge part of my life.

Communication is about sharing ideas and information. If the other person cannot understand or at least grasp the feeling of what is being said, how is it helping? If we cannot read the words, the note has no value! To try to promote Love, compassion and liberation, does not serve the other if we continually speak in jargon. The Buddha shared the Dhamma by his presence and by speaking in his own language, commonly called Pali, to his own countrymen and women, using terms and references that were familiar and relevant to their ordinary, everyday lives. This then, was the Pure Dhamma, the way to show that liberation is not something special and outside the bounds of human possibility, but is available to all in this very moment. He reminded us that the Dhamma discourse should rouse and inspire the disciple to further practice. It should lift and support the disciple in practice. How can this be achieved if the disciple does not know what the teacher is really speaking about? When confusion and misunderstanding is present, Dhamma is lost - religion, politics and social standing is born. Once we cultivate a special way of speaking we have missed the point of language and are no longer communicating honestly. We are no longer sharing ourselves with others, we are presenting something special, something exclusive something outside our ordinary human experience. This is only a place for ego enhancement, not the true humility of the teacher.

Dhamma cannot be taught, it can only be shared. It manifests from the heart that is not confused by appearances or language. It is a communication beyond words, and is shown in every moment by the quality of our life. When Dhamma is well established there is nothing to say and nothing to do. The delusion of a separate and independent self has dissolved and only 'beingness,' is present. How will we now speak about this? Live with love and be aware. Beyond that there are just more noises in the air, more scratches on a piece of paper.

The Dhamma life is a life of love,
compassion, wisdom and self responsibility.

Conditions, conditions

One time on retreat a woman came to my room about an hour before we were due to begin and spoke to me. She had just seen the programme and was alarmed by the fact that we rise at five o'clock in the morning. "But Michael," she said, "I can't get up at five o'clock in the the morning." I was surprised to hear such a thing before we had even begun the retreat and so I asked her why she felt that. "Why?" she replied throwing her arms in the air, "Because I will go mad!"

Dhamma is the greatest gift we can give ourselves, but in order to receive this gift we have to make an effort. We have to surrender into life. Our usual way of being is to apply conditions to everything we do, and when we don't get what we want, we suffer in one way or another. On retreat the most important thing is to arrive without conditions and demands as to how the retreat should be, but simply surrender into the programme. In this way the programme will lift us and support our practice. How will we ever see the nature of the mind if we continue to blindly follow it wherever it goes? It is exactly the same situation with life. As much as we may want to control everyone and everything in every moment, we are always going to be unable to do it! The cause of our happiness and unhappiness is not the outside world but only ourselves and our relationship with this mind. The teaching and practice of Dhamma therefore is to see, know and accept this mind as it manifests moment after moment, but never be a victim to it. We have to wake up to the reality of life and not just make our sleep as comfortable as possible. As pleasant as that can be on many occasions, it can never completely satisfy us as the mind itself never rests in it's endless quest for perfection in a self created universe that, in the end, can never be perfect. The way out of this tangle is wisdom. Not blind faith or belief, but wisdom. To cultivate the quality of mind that can see, know and accept the reality of each moment and be at peace with it. The mind that can accept and respond to even the things that are difficult without complaint or suffering. The mind that can be generous and loving without fear. The mind that makes no conditions about the world it experiences, but responds lovingly and fearlessly in every moment. This, then is the liberation.

Everything you want you already have,
just look behind your fears.

Years of Dhamma

For all of my many years of training, the only thing I ever wanted was to be a worthy disciple of my teacher, the Buddha and the Dhamma. I see now that even when I was instructed to teach it was only the continuation of my own training, as we always take care of those things that are precious to us, and for me Dhamma was, and is, everything. It is true that as we teach we learn, and since those very early days, sitting in small rooms sharing Dhamma with groups of interested people, throughout my many years in India to now, sharing from country to country through the modern technology of Skype, it has been my own great joy. One time during those early years someone came to train with me. At the beginning they were very enthusiastic as is usual, and meditated a lot as well as asking many questions and listening to Dhamma talks. After three months this person arrived at my door and looking me directly in the eye said, "Now I have the same understanding as you," and left, never to be seen again.

The way we see our true Dhamma understanding is to look at the quality of our life. Here if we are honest, we will see everything. Carrying and repeating the words of the teacher is not the same as having the spontaneous understanding of them. This usually takes many years of consistent effort, letting go, letting go, letting go. The unlearning and deconditioning process of Dhamma demands a true dedication and a prioritising of practice. Memorising a few quotations and scriptural verses will never be enough. If we really have the same understanding as the teacher our life will manifest the same qualities as the teacher, after all, at the place of liberation we are all exactly the same. The heart expresses itself with love, compassion, joy and equanimity, naturally and spontaneously in every moment and in every situation. When this is the manifestation of our life we are able to say that we have the same understanding as the teacher, but in this moment which part of us would ever even think such a thing? Dhamma life is not a contest. Dhamma sharing is not a lesson to give others. When there is the true understanding of the emptiness of a substantial self, who is there to stand above others and say, 'I know, listen to me?' For myself, I have no teaching to give, only the sharing of the most precious thing in my life, as it was shared with me for so many years.

Dhamma is sharing without conditions. Love is sharing without demands. Wisdom is a life of powerful and loving responses to each and every situation. This, in the end, is Dhamma.

With awareness we see,
with love we accept,
with wisdom we respond.
This is the whole of the Dhamma.

About the author

Michael Kewley is the former Buddhist monk, Paññadipa, and now an internationally acclaimed master of Dhamma, presenting courses and meditation retreats throughout the world.

A disciple of the late Sayadaw Rewata Dhamma, he teaches solely on the instruction of his own master, to share the Dhamma, in the spirit of the Buddha, so that all beings might benefit.

> Full biography and further teachings of
> Michael can be found at:
> www.puredhamma.org

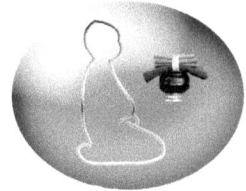

Also by Michael Kewley.

Published by
Pannadipa Books

Higher Than Happiness
Vipassana, the way to an awakened life
Not This
Life changing magic
Walking the Path
The Other Shore
The Reality of Kamma
Life is not personal
Nimm das leben nicht persönlich
The Dhammapada
Knöpfe in der Dana Box

www.ingramcontent.com/pod-product-compliance
Ingram Content Group UK Ltd.
Pitfield, Milton Keynes, MK11 3LW, UK
UKHW021257180426
11947UKWH00015B/894